**W9-BAR-929**

ALSO BY JANET MALCOLM

*Diana and Nikon: Essays on Photography*

*Psychoanalysis: The Impossible Profession*

*In the Freud Archives*

*The Journalist and the Murderer*

*The Purloined Clinic*

*The Silent Woman: Sylvia Plath and Ted Hughes*

# THE CRIME OF
# SHEILA
# McGOUGH

# THE CRIME OF
# SHEILA
# McGOUGH

*by*

# JANET MALCOLM

Alfred A. Knopf    *New York*    1999

THIS IS A BORZOI BOOK
PUBLISHED BY ALFRED A. KNOPF, INC.

www.randomhouse.com

Library of Congress Cataloging-in-Publication Data
Malcolm, Janet.
The crime of Sheila McGough / by Janet Malcolm. — 1st ed.
p.   cm.
ISBN 0-375-40508-9 (hc)
1. McGough, Sheila—Trials, litigation, etc.  2. Trials (Fraud)—
Virginia—Alexandria.  3. Criminal justice, Administration of.
I. Title.
KF224.M357M35   1999
345.73'0263—dc21          98-48635
CIP

Manufactured in the United States of America

First Edition

*To Gardner*

He didn't answer. He rather said: "It is possible to think this: without a reference point there is meaninglessness. But I wish you'd understand that without a reference point you're in the real."

—Sharon Cameron,
*Beautiful Work: A Meditation on Pain*

# PART I

THE TRANSCRIPTS of trials at law—even of routine criminal prosecutions and tiresome civil disputes—are exciting to read. They record contests of wit and will that have the stylized structure and dire aura of duels before dawn. The reader feels as if he has been brought to the clearing and can smell the wet grass; at the end, as the sky begins to show more light and the doctor is stanching a wound, he takes away a sense of having attended a momentous, if brutal and inconclusive, occasion.

Trial transcripts have no author, but they read as if someone wrote them. Their plot revolves around two struggles. One struggle is between two competing narratives for the prize of the jury's vote. The other is the struggle of narrative itself against the constraints of the rules of evidence, which seek to arrest its flow and blunt its force. The word "objection" appears in the transcript perhaps more frequently than any other, and betokens the story-spoiling function of the law. The law is the guardian of the ideal of unmediated truth, truth stripped bare of the ornament of narration; the judge, its representative, adjudicates between each lawyer's attempt to use the rules of evidence to dismantle the story of the other, while preserving the integrity of his own. The story that can best withstand the attrition of the rules of evidence is the story that wins.

The law's demand that witnesses speak "nothing but the truth" is a demand no witness can fulfill, of course, even with

God's help. It runs counter to the law of language, which pro-
scribes unregulated truth-telling and requires that our utter-
ances tell coherent, and thus never merely true, stories. This
law—with its servants ellipsis, condensation, presupposition,
syllogism—makes human communication possible. It also provides trial lawyers with endless opportunities for discrediting
opposing witnesses. In the discourse of real life—life outside
the courtroom—the line between narration and lying is a pretty
clear one. As we talk to each other, we constantly make little
adjustments to the cut of the truth in order to comply with our
listeners' expectation that we will guide them to the point of
what we are saying. If we spoke the whole truth, which has no
point—which is, in fact, shiningly innocent of a point—we
would quickly lose our listeners' attention. The person who
insists on speaking the whole truth, who painfully spells out
every last detail of an action and interrupts his wife to say it
was Tuesday, not Wednesday, and the gunman was wearing a
Borsalino, not a fedora, is not honored for his honesty but is
shunned for his tiresomeness. In a courtroom, however, he
would be one of the few people who could withstand cross-
examination, who would not be caught in the web of one or
another of the small untruths most of us mechanically tell in
order that human communication be a swift, clear river rather
than a sluggish, obstructed stream.

    As I was rereading the transcript of a criminal trial held in
federal court in Alexandria, Virginia, in the fall of 1990, my
attention was caught by an example of one such narrativizing
untruth uttered by a prosecution witness named Frank Manfredi, as he was being questioned by the prosecutor, Mark J.
Hulkower. Hulkower was eliciting from Manfredi the history
of a business transaction that lay at the heart of his case against
the defendant, a forty-eight-year-old lawyer named Sheila
McGough. The exchange between Hulkower and Manfredi
went as follows:

Q: Directing your attention to May 1986, did you have occasion at that time to become involved in a transaction for the purchase of insurance companies?

A: Yes.

Q: How did you learn of that opportunity?

A: I saw an advertisement in the *Wall Street Journal*.

Q: With whom were you put in touch?

A: I dialed the number that was in the ad. At that time I spoke, either the first call or the second call, to Mr. Bob Bailes.

The ad in question, which ran in the *Wall Street Journal* on Friday, June 13, 1986, read:

INSURANCE COMPANIES FOR SALE

Trustee in Bankruptcy is selling the stock of 17 Insurance Companies, which is owned and controlled by a corporation in bankruptcy under Chapter 11. Please write S. S. Smith, attorney and Trustee, P. O. Box 1474, Abingdon, VA 24210.

Manfredi's testimony about the ad, set side by side with the ad itself, offers an instance of demonstrable falsehood. The ad proves that Manfredi spoke falsely when he said he "dialed the number that was in the ad," since no number appears in the ad. Common sense tells us that Manfredi probably forgot the uninteresting intervening steps he had had to take (writing to the attorney, S. S. Smith, or calling Information) before he could speak to the insurance companies' owner, Mr. Bob Bailes. Memory functions as a ruthless editor of God's long-winded truth. It cuts through tedious, insignificant detail. Trial lawyers cynically rely on this function to help them impeach witnesses under cross-examination; much of the work of preparing for trial goes into the search for traces of memory's blue pencil with which to brand opposing witnesses liars. In this case, the defense lawyers, Gary Kohlman and Mark Rochon, did not so brand Manfredi; his testimony about "the number that was in the ad" went by unchallenged and unnoticed. I had dug up the ad out of a writer's inquisitiveness, a storyteller's wish to go back to the origins of the story, a journalist's habit of lingering in empty rooms on the off chance that a secret door will give way under accidental pressure.

Kohlman and Rochon lost the trial. Their client was found guilty of fourteen out of fifteen counts of felony on Wednesday, November 21, 1990, the day before Thanksgiving (the jury, evidently needing the afternoon hours for shopping for cranberries and canned pumpkin, reached its verdict by lunchtime after six hours of deliberation). She was sentenced to three years in prison, and after she lost her appeal she served two and a half years of the time. About a year after her release, in the winter of 1996, she wrote to me and said:

> I was a defense lawyer who irritated some federal judges and federal prosecutors in the course of defending a client. The federal prosecutors in my hometown [Alexandria, Virginia] investigated me for four years, and when they failed to turn up anything illegal in what I was doing, they made up some crimes for me and found people to support them with false testimony. . . . I didn't commit any of the 14 felonies I was convicted of. The U.S. Government office in Alexandria "framed" me.

After poking and peering at this case for over a year, I have come to the conclusion that Sheila McGough's summary is an accurate one. It seems scarcely possible that in this country someone could go to prison for merely being irritating, but as far as I can make out, this is indeed what happened to Sheila McGough. She is a woman of almost preternatural honesty and decency. She can also be maddeningly tiresome and stubborn.

As one looks at her disastrous confrontation with authority, one thinks of Antigone. And yet when one studies the case closely, one sees that she is not Antigone but Creon. What nettled the government about Sheila McGough was not her flouting of the law but her driving of it into the ground—her legal fundamentalism and literalism.

Under our system of justice, a person accused of a crime is entitled to a defense that is equal in power to the attack of the prosecution and to all the prerogatives of respect and consideration due to a contestant in a match of equals. (Defendants who are in jail appear in court in suits and ties or dresses, rather than in prison uniforms, to betoken this parity.) If he wins and is acquitted, he is taken back into society and his citizen's rights are fully restored to him. But should he lose, he is ejected from society, his rights are stripped from him, and he is subjected to punishment. Although there is wide disagreement about the degree of punishment that should be meted out to unsuccessful criminal defendants—who become criminals directly the verdict is read—there is general acceptance of the idea of punishment. There is also agreement that the game of trials is played for keeps and that when there is a conviction, it should hold. There is the possibility of appeal, but the system is weighted to protect the conviction. Society wants closure and provides itself with it. A conviction is extremely hard to overturn; if it were easy, the result would be an endless round of rematches.

Sheila McGough represented Bob Bailes—the man who placed the *Wall Street Journal* ad—in federal court in Alexandria in the late summer of 1986 against the charge of giving false information to a bank in order to secure a loan; she lost the case, and Bailes was convicted and sentenced to five years in prison. Two years later, while still in prison, he was brought to trial again, this time in Charlotte, North Carolina, for an older and more serious offense—"a scheme to defraud" he had attempted to carry out in the early eighties. He was convicted once again and sentenced to an additional twenty-five years.

The crime that Sheila McGough was convicted of in 1990 was the crime of not letting go, of not accepting the unwritten law of closure.

After her client went to prison, she continued defending him as if nothing had happened, as if he were still a person with rights rather than a convict without any, and as if the appeal stage of a case were the same as the pretrial and trial stages. She refused to accept the guilty verdict (and, subsequently, verdicts). Although such refusals are not unknown in life as well as in fiction, in most instances lawyers who file appeals for convicted felons don't expect to prevail. After the appeal fails—as it usually does—they withdraw their attention; they, too, need to close the book on the case and move on. But Sheila McGough never withdrew her attention from Bob Bailes. She remained at his side and fought for him as if he were Alfred Dreyfus, instead of the small-time con man, with an unfortunate medical history and an interesting imagination, that he was.

The judge who sentenced him to twenty-five years in prison addressed him thus: "Mr. Bailes, you have led a life of nothing but fraud and perjury for at least the last thirteen years. If you'd devoted the talents you have and the energy you have expended in these falsifications [to honest enterprise], you'd probably be making a million dollars a year now instead of going to jail." This is a common idea about con men—which misses the point about them. Con men are not businessmen manqués. They are not businessmen at all. They are in an entirely different line of work. They are not called con artists for nothing; they are called con artists precisely in recognition of the qualities they share with regular artists, which are: (1) love of solitude; (2) love of freedom; (3) dislike of authority; and (4) extraordinary powers of daydreaming.

The clientele for con art has never been large; it is a specialized clientele, made up of people who are dreamers in their own right, people for whom the fantasy of getting something for nothing, or close to nothing, is so powerful that it frees them from the constraints of common sense. Common sense is the enemy of art, as we all know. The spell of any work of art can be shattered by the sound of the nasty little voice saying, "But this is ridiculous." The clientele for Bob Bailes's art was smaller and more specialized still: he was a kind of con man's con man. The "scheme to defraud" for which he was convicted in North Carolina was a sort of Duchampian meditation on con art itself. Bailes claimed to possess certain extraordinary insurance companies, which were governed by charters granted in the 1890s, when insurance was not yet subject to the state regulations by which policyholders are now protected. He said he had legal documents that empowered the owners of these wonderful companies to sell insurance as if they were living in the lawless past, free of all regulation. The people Bailes offered his unregulated insurance companies to weren't credulous old ladies but spiritual colleagues of his. The idea of a company whose extraordinary value lay in its resemblance to an elevator that some fluke of history has exempted from all safety regulations could appeal only to people who themselves functioned on a high level of cynicism and amorality.

Since the early 1980s, Bailes had been offering his sardonic pieces through a leading con-art dealer—the Classifieds section of the *Wall Street Journal*. (The FBI, I was told by a former agent, keeps an agent assigned to this section.) In early June 1986, soon after Sheila McGough took him on as a client and was preparing his defense against the bank fraud charges, Bailes placed what was to be the last of his *Wall Street Journal* ads—the one that Frank Manfredi answered. By June 18, Manfredi and his partner, Francis Boccagna, had signed a contract with Bailes to buy two insurance companies for $900,000 apiece, with a down payment of $75,000 for both. The history of what happened next exists in two versions: the government's and Sheila McGough's. In the government's version, Sheila was Bailes's accomplice in the scam. She was the woman in the La Tour painting who tensely watches the dupe's foolish face as she cuts the strings of his purse. Her role in the scam, as Hulkower outlined it to the jury, was to use the dignity of her office to lull the investors into a false sense of security. She had assured them that their $75,000 down payment would be held in escrow, he said. But then, on the very day that they wired the money to her attorney trust account, she removed it and gave it to Bailes, keeping $5,000 for herself. And when the deal collapsed under the weight of its improbability, the down payment was nowhere to be found. Hulkower called it the "escrow scam."

Sheila's version of what happened was never heard at trial. Defendants in criminal trials often don't testify. Their lawyers fear that what will happen to them under cross-examination— the beating they will take—will outweigh any gain. In Sheila's case, however, the decision not to testify was made not by her lawyers but by Sheila herself, out of protectiveness for her client. If she had testified in her own behalf, she would have been cross-examined and inevitably forced to answer questions about Bailes, and her answers might have been harmful to Bailes. To save herself at her client's expense was unthinkable.

AFTER READING Sheila's letter, I wrote back and proposed that we meet. Hers was not the first letter I had received from someone claiming to have been unjustly convicted—what journalist today has not received such letters? But there was something about this writer—perhaps simply that she had put the word "framed" in quotes—that drew me to her, that made me want to know more about her case. "It was a medium-sized local story," she said at the end of her letter, "and the writers around here are sure they know what happened: a naive, unmarried woman was beguiled into crime by a con man who sent roses to her law office. So no one is willing to consider another possibility and actually read the documents."

Sheila took the train up from Washington (after getting permission from her probation officer, under whose watch she would be for another year) and met me in a coffeehouse in downtown Manhattan. She was already there when I came in, sitting at a marble-top table with the look of someone who had been waiting for some time. I don't know what I expected, but it wasn't a woman who looked and sounded like one of the blandly wholesome heroines of fifties movies. She was small and blond and pretty, and her voice was fresh and girlish, formed for phrases like "Gee whillikers!" and inflected by habits of unremitting good sportsmanship. She looked younger than her fifty-four years. Prison had evidently not broken or marked her. With her pale, translucent skin and single-strand pearl necklace and decorous navy-blue suit, she might have been the director of a small foundation or a corporate wife from Scarsdale, in town for a matinee. She talked almost uninterruptedly for the two hours of our meeting. Bailes had died the previous year, she told me, so she was finally free of her burden of silence; she could speak about him to an outsider without fear of doing him harm. However, I couldn't get a purchase on most of what she said. Too much had happened and it had been locked up in her too long for it to assume the shape of a comprehensible narrative. But Sheila, in any case, was not interested in telling a plausible and persuasive and interesting story. She was out for the bigger game of imparting a great number of wholly accurate and numbingly boring facts.

I was to realize over my months of meeting with her and talking with her on the telephone that she was unlike any other journalistic subject I had ever encountered. The journalistic subject is normally someone with a story to tell; you might even say to sell. Sheila's refusal (or inability) to tell a story obviated the usual journalistic task of dismantling a well-made story. With Sheila, the task, on the contrary, was to try to coax a story from the morass of her guileless and incontinent speech. Her lawyers had evidently not been up to the task. To win their case, they needed to tell a story at least as compelling as the prosecution's—the story, as Hulkower neatly summarized it in his opening statement, "of what happens when an attorney violates the first rule of criminal defense and crosses the line from representation of the criminal to participation in his crimes." But no powerful counterstory was ever told by Kohlman and Rochon. With their hands tied by the double bonds of the rules of evidence and the stubborn silence of their client, they could do little more than rush around putting out little fires in wastebaskets as the entire building burned to the ground. When a powerful counterstory finally emerged—the story told by Sheila's appeal lawyer, Stuart Abrams—the day for powerful counterstories was past. Like the convicted Bailes, the convicted Sheila was beyond rescue by narrative; she was beyond the heavy door that can be opened only by the most massive assault on it of brute fact. Abrams accused the government of using perjured testimony to win its case and offered evidence of lying by government witnesses that would have given a jury something to think about but did not move the stony appeals court, which reverses only when it must. Abrams's story stirred my reporter's imagination. I have daydreamed of taking his work the step further needed to prove that Sheila was convicted by false evidence. But my fantasy that Abrams and I would work hand in hand to clear Sheila has not been fulfilled. Unlike Sheila, Abrams knows when to let go, and he has let Sheila go. Most of my calls to him go unanswered, but as a favor to Sheila, he allowed me two interviews.

Abrams is a former government attorney who works in private practice in New York. He is a quiet, mild-mannered, very intelligent, deliberately colorless man. He seems to be kind and to have a sense of humor, which he thinks it wise to suppress when in the presence of a journalist. There is something old-fashioned about his reserve and caution. When I try to remember what he looks like, I think of a faded photograph of a man taken in a suburban train station on a gray morning. I don't know why I think of him as a commuter; perhaps because something about him evokes the mysterious, depressed men in John Cheever's stories.

I went to see Abrams in his small, plain office in a big office building in the East Forties a few days after meeting Sheila in the coffeehouse. She had given him permission—as she gave all her other lawyers permission—to breach client-attorney privilege in speaking to me. "It's a very strange case," he said. "I don't understand why the government brought it. It has never added up to me. I have always had the feeling that there was another story that didn't come out at trial. Sheila did not seem to me to be a crook. And the people she supposedly defrauded weren't widows or orphans. It's hard for me to see them as victims."

The people Abrams finds it hard to see as victims are: Frank Manfredi, a forty-nine-year-old disbarred lawyer, currently serving a four-to-seven-year sentence for grand larceny in a state prison; Alan Morris, a fifty-year-old disbarred lawyer, recently released from prison; Francis Boccagna, a thirty-two-year-old loan broker and erstwhile partner of Manfredi's; Philip Zinke, a fifty-seven-year-old career criminal and government informer; and Kirkpatrick MacDonald, an affluent fifty-eight-year-old investment banker. These were the men involved in the deal that was the centerpiece of Hulkower's case against Sheila. Hulkower put it this way:

> Now, the government doesn't contend that there was anything wrong with Sheila McGough representing Bob Bailes on criminal charges. It's what criminal defense attorneys do. But the evidence will show, ladies and gentlemen, that what led to her downfall and what led to these proceedings today is that instead of remaining at arms' distance from Bob Bailes, and remaining Bob Bailes' criminal lawyer, Sheila McGough came too close to Bob Bailes, and began to handle his business affairs, and as the business affairs of a con man like Bob Bailes

involve conning people, so too did the defendant, Sheila McGough, become involved in the con schemes.

*What led to her downfall.* Hulkower was anticipating, of course. Sheila's downfall came only with the guilty verdict. But he was also echoing what he knew to be an assumption of the jury. In her letter to me, Sheila had said she was framed—but in a sense, everyone who is brought to trial, criminal or civil, is framed. For while the law speaks of a presumption of innocence, it knows full well that the accused is weighed down under a burden extremely difficult to get out from under. The deck is stacked against the accused. An accusation has enormous psychological clout. Once someone is accused of a crime or misdeed, he begins to burn with a kind of radioactivity. The story of wrongdoing that the prosecutor or the plaintiff's lawyer tells the jury is a fleshing out of the jury's preconception. The task of the defense is not to clear the accused (that is impossible; it is too late for that) but to attack the accusers—to show that the plaintiff or the government's witnesses are even worse than the accused.

Kohlman and Rochon could deliver only glancing blows to their opponents. Hulkower's narrative held. Its linchpin was the testimony of Manfredi, Boccagna, and Morris, each of whom said that Sheila had given them verbal assurance that the $75,000 would be held in escrow. Sheila's story—the one she didn't tell in court—is that she never gave them any such assurance.

Before hearing more of her story, we need to have a firmer grasp of the transaction. When Manfredi "dialed the number that was in the ad" and told Bailes that he wanted to buy two insurance companies, he meant something a little different by the word "buy" from what the rest of us mean. His lawyer, Alan Morris, who appeared as a witness at the trial, explained that Manfredi and his partner, Boccagna, "were going to what we call 'flip' the transaction to an ultimate buyer." Hulkower, who was examining Morris, asked: "So they were going to buy and then turn around and sell?" Morris delicately corrected him: "They were going to try to make a buyer actually buy without them having to expend any money." The "ultimate buyer" Manfredi and Boccagna found was a woman in Buffalo, New York, named Bernice Kelly; but at the eleventh hour, for reasons unknown—or reasons Manfredi, Boccagna, and Morris thought it best to leave unstated—Kelly withdrew from the deal, and exited forever from its history. At trial, Kohlman, looking where he could for soft places in the prosecution's case, suggested that Bernice Kelly never existed, since no contracts with her signature—or, indeed, any paper trace of her at all—could be produced. But this went nowhere and had no point, since nothing hinged on whether Bernice Kelly was real or not. (I myself believe in her and see her as a rather heavy woman with a flushed face and dark curly hair, sitting at a table in a bar in Buffalo with a man who is watching a hockey game on television. She gets up and goes to a phone in a narrow passageway near the toilets and tells Boccagna the deal is off. When she returns to the table, the man puts an arm around her without taking his eyes off the television screen.)

For Manfredi and Boccagna, it was imperative that a new ultimate buyer be found (before a restive Bailes snatched the companies away and sold them to someone else on his waiting list), and he appeared on cue, in the form of the rogue Philip Zinke. Zinke, like Manfredi and Boccagna (and perhaps Kelly), had no intention of parting with any of his own money. Among con artists, allowing money to leave your hands for even a moment when it can leave someone else's is a violation of a rule of art, an insult to yourself and to your calling. Zinke, as Manfredi testified, "was one of Frank's [Boccagna's] individuals." Boccagna was only twenty years old at the time of the transaction. A year earlier, he had dropped out of NYU, after the death of his father, to go into business for himself, as a real estate speculator and loan broker, with money his father had left him. Boccagna took out an ad in the *New York Times* offering loans, and Zinke, who was looking for funds "for some deal he had with some copper mine" (as Boccagna later testified in a deposition), answered it. No loan was made—Zinke wanted more money than Boccagna was prepared to lend—but when, in passing, Boccagna mentioned Bailes's insurance charters to Zinke, "his eyes lit up," and he said he would buy the two companies. He then called a man he had once worked with at Lehman Brothers, Kirkpatrick MacDonald, and offered him a partnership in the deal. MacDonald not only accepted but was persuaded to put up Zinke's half of the $75,000 down payment as well.

The patsy—someone who was actually going to part with money—had finally appeared. Unfortunately for Sheila, he was a patsy without a patsy's philosophical bent. When he realized that he had been cheated, he didn't shrug and sadly stumble away in the direction of his next disaster. He moved heaven and earth to retrieve his loss and to strike back at those who had tried to take advantage of him. MacDonald was a harsh and punitive man, a sort of Roger Chillingworth. Being made a fool of was not his style, and he went into manic action. He telephoned the FBI in Alexandria, Virginia, told his story, and was encouraged to fly to Washington to incriminate an unsuspecting Bailes. At a restaurant called Hogates, over lobster and beer, MacDonald, wearing a concealed tape recorder, drew out the loquacious con man. The transcript of the conversation, which became an exhibit at Sheila's trial, contains this typical passage:

> MACDONALD: What have you found these companies are worth when you sell them to people? What do they end up selling for? Licensed to do business everywhere, all kinds of business in every state? That's real attractive to me.

BAILES: Well . . . we sold one for three million dollars to a guy in Texas, and he sold it for 7½ million to people who turned around and sold it to a big company for 12½ million.

MACDONALD: Wow.

BAILES: I don't know what they're worth. Who can say? It's worth what people pay for it.

The next morning, MacDonald was debriefed at FBI headquarters in Alexandria. Then, with the tape recorder and microphone once again in covert place, he went across town to see Sheila in her office. For the first fifteen or twenty minutes of his visit, he egged her on, as he had egged Bailes on, to incriminate herself with false claims about the insurance charters, but she did not oblige him. She said she knew very little about them, and that it was Bailes and S. S. Smith that he ought to talk to. MacDonald then dropped his mask and demanded that she give him back his $75,000. Sheila did not oblige him here, either, and in March 1987 MacDonald sued her for the return of his money. (There would have been no point in suing Bailes—who was now in prison and had no insurance.) The following fall, just as the case was to be tried, he received a settlement payment of $75,000 plus interest from Sheila's Errors and Omissions insurance. But this was not enough for MacDonald. He needed to further punish and humiliate the woman he had already brought to her knees. "My interest . . . is to see this lady put out of business," he wrote in a letter of October 1988 to the Virginia State Bar, seeking to get her disbarred. "She is a loathsome sort and as a citizen I wish to get her off the streets." He told the bar association the history of the suit he had been "forced to institute" against Sheila and of his "close touch" with the FBI and the U.S. Attorney in Alexandria, who "are completely aware of Ms. McGough's background and activities and have on numerous occasions told me that she would be indicted. This has not happened yet due, I was told, to the fact that there are bigger fish in Washington waters (which I believe). Time, therefore, to at least get you fellows on her case." But even after the government, sated on its big fish, turned to Sheila and dispatched her with a lazy paw, MacDonald did not let up on his quarry. "The court should be severe in its sentence," he wrote to Mark Hulkower a month before Sheila's sentencing, "not only because of the nature of Ms. McGough's crime—in itself an outrageous insult to the public trust—but also because of her apparent lack of contrition, which shows an obvious character defect." MacDonald concluded his letter to Hulkower rather weirdly: "Whatever time in prison she receives, she should also be subject to a very substantial amount of community service. This avenue of punishment has very positive effects, I believe, in helping people such as Ms. McGough to change their outlooks and eventually return to society."

Sheila had been sent a copy of MacDonald's complaint to the Virginia State Bar, and she responded to it, Sheila fashion, point by point, often straying into byways of deep irrelevancy but sometimes speaking with uncharacteristic directness, as when she declared in no uncertain terms that "I did not agree at any time to be an escrow agent or to hold money until certain conditions had been fulfilled." This is what never got said at trial because of Sheila's refusal to testify. If she had said it, and the jury had believed her, the outcome would have been different. The "escrow scam" was the heart of the government's case, and if its narration had faltered, the rest of the case would have collapsed. In her reply to MacDonald's complaint, Sheila also made some pointed remarks about her settlement with him. "My counsel had recommended settlement as a way of avoiding the 'embarrassment' of a trial that would taint me by association with these people. . . . I thought at the time it was a cowardly thing to do and made me in a moral sense the accomplice to a fraud against my carrier." Sheila had agreed to settle only on the day of the trial and only after the judge, Albert Bryan, Jr.—the same judge who, by apparent coincidence, was to preside over her criminal trial—said he wished the case settled. She has told me that she considers settling with MacDonald a failure of nerve and a major blunder, and she is right. Although the settlement agreement contained no admission of fault on Sheila's part, the fact that it granted to MacDonald the full sum of $75,000 could be taken as a tacit confession of guilt, as Hulkower lost no opportunity to point out.

The chronicler of the transaction that introduced Sheila to her nemesis begins to lose his bearings soon after the fatal down payment was wired to Sheila's account. At this juncture, he is like a motorist driving on a clear night who suddenly runs into a stretch of swirling, low-lying mist and must creep along using his dimmed headlights to try to see. The transaction dematerialized shortly after the down payment was made, but it isn't clear how or why. MacDonald, Zinke, Manfredi, Boccagna, and Morris have all testified about this murky moment, but their accounts, as well as lacking in explanatory power, are so contradictory that historical reconstruction based on them is impossible.

Historical reconstruction in all cases gives rise to structures that are more like ruins than proper buildings; there is never enough solid building material and always too much dust. But in the case of the collapse of the Manfredi-Boccagna-Kelly-Zinke-MacDonald transaction with Bailes there is (perhaps appropriately enough) almost nothing but dust. We don't know what happened, why it happened, who said what to whom. All we know is that by the end of the summer Zinke had disappeared; Manfredi, Boccagna, and Morris had slunk away; Bailes was on his way to prison; and MacDonald had hired a high-powered lawyer named Michael Wyatt to represent him in his suit against Sheila.

HISTORY IS a story chafing against the bonds of documentary fact. Trial lawyers are a species of historian who work in a more charged atmosphere and for higher stakes than do regular, clientless historians, but who are part of the same guild of hobbled narrators. (Biographers and journalists are other members.) How Mark Hulkower, in spite of extremely serious constraints, narrated his story of Sheila's role in the "escrow scam" offers an instructive glimpse into the workings of historical method and illustrates its inevitable alliance with the forces of purposive storytelling against those of aimless truth-seeking:

> Now the defendant worked closely with Bob Bailes in this scheme. Her role was to tell potential investors, people who were looking into the possibility of buying one of these insurance companies, victims . . . that if they sent to her account, her attorney trust account, a refundable deposit to hold one of those insurance companies, she would retain the deposit in her attorney trust account, in her escrow account, and you will hear that an attorney trust account is a special account attorneys at law have for holding money for people, just for that purpose. Sheila McGough would tell the investors that she would hold the money in [her] account and then having induced the investors to turn over the money to her, she would disburse it. . . . Witness after witness will come here, ladies and gentlemen, and tell you how Sheila McGough deceived them.

The document that most heavily taxed Hulkower's powers as a storyteller and threatened to spoil his narrative of the "escrow scam"—as it had already discomfited MacDonald's lawyer in his civil suit against Sheila—was that most mundane but irrefutable agent of fact, a telephone bill. Alan Morris's telephone bill for July 1986 had strayed into the discovery of the MacDonald suit (Morris had carelessly left it in a sheaf of documents he was required to submit to the lawyers on both sides) and couldn't be dislodged, like the ledge of granite that emerges beneath a building site and must be accepted and incorporated into the architect's plans. The bill revealed that the crucial telephone conversation in which Sheila was supposed to have "induced the investors to part with their money" by assuring Morris that the $75,000 down payment would be held in escrow was only one minute long. It rendered worthless—and perjurious—the testimony of Frank Manfredi in a deposition taken a week earlier, when the telephone bill had not yet surfaced and Manfredi had felt free to indulge his habit of compulsive untruthfulness. Manfredi drew a vivid scene: He spoke of sitting in Morris's office in Garden City on July 15— the day before MacDonald's money was wired to Sheila's account—and listening to Morris converse with Sheila on a speakerphone, which permitted him to hear both sides of the conversation. According to the deposition transcript, Morris read Sheila a letter (later mailed to her) that spelled out the terms of the escrow agreement. The transcript continues:

Q: Is there any doubt in your mind, Mr. Manfredi, that on the 15th Miss McGough understood that the $75,000 was to be placed in an escrow account in her name?

A: None whatsoever because this letter (indicating)—

Q: You are referring now to Exhibit 7?

A: Yes. (continuing) Was specifically read to her.

Q: To Miss McGough?

A: That is correct.

Q: In this July 15 conversation?

A: I believe it was. We had several conversations on July 15. Alan Morris read this letter to her in my presence.

Q: Verbatim?

A: Yes, because it wasn't until they said fine that we arranged to have the monies wired the following morning from, I believe, it was Morgan Guaranty.

The letter, dated July 16 and received by Sheila about a week later, read:

Dear Ms. McGough:

This will confirm my conversation of July 15, 1986 with Robert Bayliss [*sic*] regarding the above matter. At this time my clients have arranged to wire to your account the sum of $75,000.00 which represents the down payment in this transaction. Additional terms were likewise agreed on as follows:

A) Down payment will be held in your bankruptcy account until closing of this transaction. In the event closing cannot take place, except for a breach by the buyer, the down payment will be returned forthwith.

B) A certificate of good standing for all states and the District of Columbia will be delivered at closing.

C) A certificate of authority for the transaction of General Insurance, Property and Casualty, and annuities in all states including the District of Columbia will be delivered at closing.

I am sure that this meets with your approval, and hence it is hereby deemed that these terms are incorporated by reference into the contract dated June 24, 1986.

Should you have any questions, please contact me.

Very truly yours,
Alan D. Morris

When Morris's deposition was taken, a week after Manfredi's and a few days after the telephone bill had planted itself in the case like an unwanted chaperon, he was obliged to tell a different story from Manfredi's. Upon being asked whether he had read the letter to Sheila over the phone on July 15, he was forced to waffle. "I believe I may either have read or explained what I was going to write."

Q: You either read or paraphrased?
A: I don't believe that I read the letter because I had not drafted it. Many times you draft things and it is not typed until the following day. I indicated what I was doing, relative only to the down payment, nothing else.

By the time of the criminal trial, Morris had tidied up his story; he saw that the letter of July 16 and the one-minute phone call could not be reconciled. Under Hulkower's careful questioning, Morris testified: "I called up Ms. McGough's law office and the conversation was just, I am just confirming the fact that you are going to be holding the money in escrow, the $75,000 coming down tomorrow. There was no objection. That was the end of the conversation."

Q: So that was a short conversation?
A: Very short.

The letter of July 16 was of enormous interest to Hulkower (as it had been to Wyatt), because it was a piece of paper that actually said the down payment would be held in Sheila's account until the closing of the deal. But unfortunately for the inner consistency of the narrative of the "escrow scam," the letter isn't quite what it ought to be. It doesn't say, "Dear Ms. McGough: This will confirm *our* conversation," but refers only to a conversation with Bailes. When looked at closely, the letter would seem, if anything, to confirm Sheila's contention that she had not spoken with Morris at all on July 15. Had she done so, would not the letter have referred to the conversation? In the hands of a lesser craftsman, this inconsistency, and the inconsistencies between the depositions and the trial testimonies of Morris, Manfredi, and Boccagna, might have seriously impaired the narrative of the "escrow scam." But in the capable hands of Hulkower, the narrative beautifully held. Hulkower simply wouldn't allow the inconsistencies to impede the progress of his story, and Kohlman and Rochon were evidently unprepared to stem its flow. When Kohlman cross-examined Manfredi, instead of confronting him with the lie he told in his deposition, he merely rubbed his nose in the felonies he had been sent to prison for—felonies that Hulkower had preemptively set before the jury and that the judge finally grew tired of hearing about. "Mr. Hulkower, you have brought out that he forged somebody's name, and that he took somebody else's money that he wasn't supposed to. He has admitted that. And he is not on trial here. So why don't we move on?"

Sheila's version of what happened—the story that never got told at trial, and that I was able to pry from her only with the greatest difficulty—was this: She had but the vaguest sense of what the Manfredi-Boccagna-Kelly-Zinke-MacDonald-Bailes transaction was about. At the time, her attention was anxiously focused on the preparation of her defense of Bailes in the bank fraud case, which was scheduled for trial on July 28 and which she did not feel prepared to argue. Bailes had parked himself in her law office, as he had habitually parked himself in the law offices of his previous lawyers (such as S. S. Smith, the attorney whose name and address—unbeknownst to him—appeared in the *Wall Street Journal* ad of June 13), and while Sheila worked on his defense, he coolly worked on his own business. Believing this business to be legitimate, Sheila tolerated his presence in her office and absently consented to the unremarkable favors he asked: the use of her telephone, of her office suite's copying and typing facilities, of her attorney trust account for the receipt of the $75,000 down payment. When the money came in, she drew it out and gave it to him, minus $5,000 he told her to keep as part of the fee he owed her. It seemed so simple and straightforward. The money was his. Allowing him to use her account had been a mere "accommodation." About five days later, she received the letter of July 16 from Morris and was baffled by it. She showed the letter to Bailes, and he took it from her and said, "This is all a lot of nonsense. I'll take care of it." "I realize now that this was a big blunder," Sheila told me. "I should have written back at once and got it down on paper that I had never agreed to hold the money. But at the time, my mind was elsewhere. It didn't seem important." As for Morris's one-minute conversation with her, she says it never happened and surmises that the one-minute charge was for a call which the receptionist in her office suite picked up while she was out.

There are loose ends in Sheila's story. She told me that she had not only agreed to Bailes's use of her account for the $75,000 payment but had welcomed the arrangement. "Since Bobby was being tried for bank fraud, and the charges came out of some forms he'd filled out, I didn't want him to go to a bank to open a new account. I didn't want him anywhere near a bank," she said. However, Bailes already *had* a bank account in Alexandria, in the name of Preferred Research, one of the companies he professed to own. When I questioned Sheila about this—about why the money hadn't been wired to that account instead of to hers—she had no answer. But even without this and other strangenesses, Sheila's story is not a good one. It seems unbelievable that someone who had a law degree could be so credulous and so careless. I happen to believe that Sheila's weak story is true and that Hulkower's strong story is off the mark. But that's because I have had the opportunity to study Sheila over time and (following the cues of Stuart Abrams) to come face-to-face with Morris and Manfredi's untruthfulness. The jury had no such opportunity.

What Sheila's case illustrates with special vividness is something all attorneys know, which is that truth is a nuisance in trial work. The truth is messy, incoherent, aimless, boring, absurd. The truth does not make a good story; that's why we have art. The prosecutor prosecuting an innocent person or the defense lawyer defending a guilty client actually have an easier task than their opposite numbers. In the unjust prosecution and in the lying defense, much of the work of narration—of transforming messy actuality into an orderly story—has already been done. The just prosecution and the defense of an innocent require a great deal more work. For truth to prevail at trial, it must be laboriously transformed into a kind of travesty of itself. Sheila's lawyers, working in haste, and receiving no help from their literal-minded client, were unable to effect this transformation.

ON A Wednesday—Ash Wednesday, as it happened—in the winter of 1996, I asked Sheila McGough an intrusive but necessary question: Had she and Bailes been lovers? At trial, Hulkower had labored mightily to establish a romantic attachment as the motive for Sheila's "criminal conduct." He produced invoices from an Alexandria flower shop for roses sent by Bailes to Sheila. He had a receptionist from Sheila's office suite testify that Sheila had started dressing better after Bailes became her client. The evidence was not overwhelming, but the alternative—that Bailes and Sheila were just another attorney and client—was hard to credit. Sheila answered, "I didn't take off my clothes with Bobby. I wasn't naked with him. We didn't have sexual intercourse." The answer was typical of her overtruthful, undercommunicative responses. It was as if she had heard only the top layer of what I had asked her, had sliced it off and left the lower half behind—the half that completes the thought and gives it its full range of implication. By denying only that she had slept with him, she seemed to be saying that she was otherwise involved with him—probably in love with him. This wasn't so, it turned out. I pressed Sheila on the point, and finally was satisfied that Hulkower's insinuations were groundless.

"Some of Bobby's business associates and some of his lawyers, and certainly all the prosecutors, have built up this theory of his fatal charm," she said, and continued, "Well, he was a nice man, and I feel bad about the way things turned out for him. He had some good qualities, in my opinion, which included courage and consideration for other people's feelings. But he wasn't what I would consider charming, and I've met a few charming men. No. A nice man.

"He had a kind of flirtatious way of dealing with women who were close to his age, as I was. When he interacted with women in their twenties he wasn't like that at all; he was much more formal. But with women in their forties—whether it was a court clerk or a secretary or me—his was an old-fashioned Southern man's way. It's now become unfashionable. As he might say, he didn't mean nothing by it. It was just a kind of courtesy. For instance, when I visited him in prison, he'd compliment me on my clothes: 'Oh, don't you look nice! Well, you just look so fresh, as if you hadn't traveled all that distance.'

"But I don't want to say, 'Oh, I would never have thought of a relationship with someone like him.' Who is 'someone like him'? He was a man not too far removed from my age group. As it happened, he wasn't my type, and I don't think I was his. But I came to have a lot of care and concern for him, and I think he had feelings of affection for me by the end of our relationship, though only he could tell you what that really meant. We were like two people stuck together in an elevator during an earthquake."

So there had been no romance; Sheila and Bobby *were* just another lawyer and client, as far as that went. But they weren't. I need to qualify this. Over time, some trace of eros finds its way into most lawyer-client relationships (as it does into most teacher-student and therapist-patient and journalist-subject relationships), and what was unusual about the Sheila-Bobby relationship was not the egregiousness but the near invisibility of this trace. The Sheila-Bobby relationship was as chaste and formal and distanced, as abstinent, as such a relationship can be. I know this from Sheila's account of it and from letters to her from Bailes that she has shown me; but above all, I know it from my own relationship with her, which is the most abstinent of any journalistic relationship I have known. With other subjects I have felt and succumbed to the pull of another's simple human need for diversion (as the subject has felt and succumbed to the pull of mine) and allowed myself to stray from the straight and narrow of the work at hand. I have flirted and horsed around with subjects. I have enjoyed myself with them as they have enjoyed themselves with me. With Sheila, there has never been any question of enjoyment. It has been all work; it has been the journalist-subject relationship taken to a kind of absurdist level of professionalism and impersonality. This is not to say it has been peaceful, however. I don't know if I've ever had a more irritating subject. I know I have never before behaved so badly to a subject. I have never before interrupted, lost patience with, spoken so unpleasantly to a subject as I have to Sheila—to my shame and vexation afterward. I have never before dreaded calling a subject on the telephone as I have dreaded calling Sheila. To my simplest question she would give an answer of such relentless length and tediousness and uncomprehending irrelevance that I could almost have wept with impatience. I took notes of these phone calls, and among them I have found little cries of despair. One of them was: "Help, help! I'm trapped talking to Sheila. She won't stop. Save me." And, reading it over, I realize anew why Sheila was prosecuted. Sheila had to be silenced. One of the fifteen charges against her was "obstruction of justice." But all the charges were a kind of front for the real offense: obstruction of movement. Sheila was an impediment that had to be removed. In her representation of Bailes she was like a trailer truck jackknifed across a highway. My outbursts of irritation at Sheila—my loss of control and subsequent feeling of contrition—were echoes of the outbursts she provoked in the judges before whom she appeared. A hearing before one of these, James Turk, of the U.S. District Court for the Western District of Virginia, gives a vivid sense of the effect she produces on people who are normally able to keep their emotions under control. Sheila herself speaks of Turk with respect and liking—she says he is a very decent and genial man—but at the hearing he could have killed her.

It took place on August 10, 1988, two months before Bailes was to stand trial for the "scheme to defraud"; two years after he had been convicted of giving false information to a bank; and *thirteen* years after he had pleaded nolo contendere to charges of fraud and tax evasion. Sheila had gone before Judge Turk to argue that the sentence imposed in the last case had been illegal.

"How is a sentence imposed that long ago illegal?" the judge asked.

"Well, Your Honor, under Rule 32(a), an illegal sentence may be corrected at any time. There is no time limit on that."

"Well, what is illegal about it?"

To the judge's increasing irritation and restiveness, Sheila laid out a strained and cumbersome narrative about how Bailes had recently been discovered to be suffering from a blood disorder, hypercalcemia, which, coupled with another affliction of his, diabetes, had caused him to plead guilty to something he hadn't done: namely, told a bank that he owned land he actually didn't own. He did own it, Sheila said, and she had a witness who would testify to this. She also had the testimony of a psychiatrist who, on the basis of the medical records Sheila had sent her, wrote that "Mr. Bailes' ability to perform tasks requiring complex analysis and decision making or detailed recollection of past events during 1970 to 1975 was substantially impaired."

The judge impatiently cut in: "But it doesn't say that it was impaired to the extent that he couldn't make decisions. This doesn't meet any test, Sheila. You know that."

"Your Honor, that's one leg of the tripod," Sheila replied, and remorselessly went over the ground again. "It's not just a matter of now we're trying to retry the thing and say, 'Well, maybe he wasn't guilty,' " she said. "That's not the point, Your Honor."

"What is the point?" the court asked.

"The point is that no rational man who had the ability to reason normally would plead guilty or nolo contendere that he falsely stated on a bank record that he didn't own six acres of land in Wise County, Virginia, when in fact he owned even a little more than that, and it could easily have been shown just by going down to the land records. That's the sort of thing that—"

The judge cut in again: "But we don't know about that. We know about his dealings. We know about Mr. Hugh Rakes from Floyd County and all of these kinds of things. He may not have even known at that time that somebody had put it in his name. You do not realize—you do not realize the type of activities that Mr. Bailes has been involved in all of these years."

Ms. McGough: Your Honor, I have to assume that in every piece of litigation, in every cause of action, that the judge that we come before is going to look at it in isolation and—

The Court: It certainly is if you have a meritorious claim and a claim to present, but this is frivolous and so the court may have to impose sanctions on you.

Ms. McGough: Your Honor, the evidence that we have indicates that this man was not competent to make that plea. That's—

The Court: Well, there is no evidence that he wasn't competent to make the plea and I'm ruling that he was competent to make the plea.

Ms. McGough: Your Honor, very well.

THE COURT: Okay, so you've lost on that point.

Ms. McGOUGH: Let me—

THE COURT: Now, what other point do you have?

Ms. McGOUGH: Let me go on to the next point, Your Honor.

Sheila's appearance before Turk is a microcosm of her entire doomed enterprise on Bailes's behalf. It illustrates the futility of her efforts to reverse the irreversible. It brings into relief the impossible purity of her position. The answer to the question "Shouldn't every case be considered in isolation?" is "Yes, but." Not "Yes," as she would like it to be. Without the thinner of common sense, the law is a toxic substance. Any system of justice must fall short of its stated ideal if it is going to function, if any case is ever to be decided rather than argued forever. Of course Sheila is "right" and the judge is "wrong." She is right that Bailes's case should be decided on its merits and not on the judge's knowledge of his past activities, of his dealings with Mr. Hugh Rakes, whoever Mr. Rakes may be, and of "all of these kinds of things." Sheila's view of justice—that it is like a person with dementia, a person who has no memory, for whom everything is grotesquely new and untainted—cannot be gainsaid; abstractly, ideally, justice is indeed demented. But practically it is a normal person with a memory. When Sheila brought out the third leg of her tripod—the absence of a verbatim record of the 1975 proceedings—Turk once again broke in indignantly:

THE COURT: He tried to do the same thing in West Virginia on a conviction over there. Mr. Bailes tried exactly the same thing. Now, I don't know whether you were representing him or not. You didn't win over there, did you?

Ms. McGOUGH: Your Honor, I don't know what you're referring to on that.

The Court: Well, Mr. Bailes knows. He pulled this exact same deal in West Virginia, trying to get a conviction over there set aside on the basis that they didn't have the record.

Ms. McGough: Your Honor, the rule states—we may not like the rule, but the rule is very clear.

The Court: Well, I'm not talking about the rule. I'm saying that he did the same thing in West Virginia. . . . He was trying to get Habeas relief on the basis that the record had been lost in West Virginia.

Ms. McGough: Well, may I suggest respectfully that this case turns on a very clear violation—

The Court: This case doesn't turn at all and there is nothing to this case.

Ms. McGough: —of Rule 11.

The Court: I've heard enough about it to know that there is absolutely nothing to this case, nothing.

Ms. McGough: Your Honor, the case law—

The Court: And I'm going to impose sanctions on you for bringing it when you finish up here.

Ms. McGough: Your Honor, but—

The Court: And I'm going to impose substantial sanctions.

Ms. McGough: Your Honor, I don't understand because I—

The Court: You can appeal it, but the court is going to impose sanctions on you.

Ms. McGough: Your Honor, I don't understand because I've done considerable research on the law of Rule 11 and 35(a) and I've gone to the trouble to get the certified records from Philadelphia.

The Court: Put them in the record because you're going to have to appeal this case because the court is going to put substantial sanctions on you.

Ms. McGOUGH: Certainly. These are records that are already in the court's own files. I don't know what this document is that has just been handed to me. . . .

The comic muse who has been guiding the course of the hearing now nudges it toward a delicious moment. The document that has "just been handed" to Sheila is nothing less than the missing verbatim record itself, which turned up in the basement of Judge Turk's court stenographer. It was in "a box of various and sundry transcripts," as the stenographer presently testified, "that had been used maybe to show typists where margins go and that sort of thing."

Sheila had sent me a copy of the transcript of the hearing before Turk, and on the last page she had pasted a little green note, which read: "After the proceedings were over, Turk calmed down and told me he had no intention of imposing sanctions." Turk was one of four judges whom the government subpoenaed to testify against Sheila at her criminal trial. He apparently bore her no ill will, and his testimony did her no great harm. "I thought that she was just trying to carry out the desires of her client," he said, "and I kept cautioning her about the fact that Mr. Bailes would manipulate people and that she ought to be very careful about these matters."


WHEN I asked Sheila my intrusive question about her relationship with Bailes, we were in her small white car, driving from Union Station to the house in Alexandria, Virginia, where she lives with her parents. She had insisted on meeting my train; she told me that a cabdriver would never find her house. As the familiar, always somewhat jarringly uninteresting vistas of Washington gave way to the more predictably bland landscape of the suburbs, Sheila told me about her first, fateful encounter with Bailes.

"In the spring of 1986, I received a collect call from Bobby from the jail in Fairfax, Virginia," she said. "He'd heard my name mentioned favorably by another inmate. So I went over. I think I may have done so that same day. He was in some distress. His health was poor. He was a diabetic who controlled his condition with insulin injections and a special diet. He wasn't getting the right food in the jail, and his condition was deteriorating. What I remember most about him that day was the combination of his physical disability—he looked sick, he had a bloated look—and his composure. Most of the clients I visited in jail were distraught and incoherent—that's a normal state. Bobby was composed and appreciative of my being there. He said he didn't understand why he had been arrested. It was a vendetta of some sort. He had a lot of enemies in business. A lot of people didn't like him. I finally learned that he was there on a fugitive warrant from North Carolina—on a courtesy hold—but nobody could tell me what the charge was. I tried to get bond for him, but it was denied. Then the magistrate said that if I signed my name and would be responsible for the bail money, he would release Bobby on his own recognizance. That's how I got him out. I don't remember what the sum was. It would have been a burden, but it wasn't all that much—a thousand dollars, maybe. What I did was something lawyers never, never do. I didn't go out of my way to tell anybody I had done that. It was just so unprofessional. But I would always do what was necessary for my clients. I hope that doesn't sound bad. I would not have committed crimes for my clients. But anything that was just risking my time and my money—if I had it—I would not hesitate to do."

When Sheila received the collect phone call from Bailes, she had been practicing law for only four years. She had come to law late. In her first profession, she had been an editor and administrator in the publications department of the Carnegie Institute. Then, at the age of thirty-nine, she took the audacious step of leaving a good job and starting to study law at the just-accredited law school of George Mason University, in Washington. She chose it, she told me, because it was inexpensive, within driving distance, and ready to admit her at once. She was a graduate of Georgetown University and could have got into a "better" law school, but she didn't want to wait the year these schools required. Upon graduation, she saw that perhaps she had made a miscalculation: none of the large Washington law firms she approached would even look at an application from a graduate of a law school as unimpressive as George Mason. So she went into practice for herself and had herself put on the list of lawyers at the Alexandria State Courthouse, from which court-appointed counsel for indigent clients is drawn.

Her motives weren't ideological. Sheila wasn't, and isn't, a lefty. Since high school, she had worked for the local Republican organization, and she was well versed in the Right's unsentimental rhetoric: she was "for law and order" and "against the coddling of criminals." "I believed that there were too many protections and procedures to help people accused of crimes," she told me. But when (for lack of other work and "to hone my skills") she started representing indigent criminal defendants, she made a complete about-face. She now felt that the protections and procedures were hardly adequate against the Goliath force of the government, and that only by extremes of lawyerly guile and toil could criminal defendants be saved from unjust convictions. She fought for each of her "poor wretches"—as she came to call the drug dealers, prostitutes, burglars, forgers, flashers, and concealers of weapons whom she drew—like an emergency-room doctor fighting for the life of a bleeding and broken accident victim. When she lost, she only shifted her operating table to the afterworld of appeal and prisoners' rights. At Sheila's criminal trial, the single effective witness for her was a poor wretch named Wayne Miller. He had just been paroled from a five-year conviction for drug dealing, and he testified to the lengths that Sheila had gone to in representing him—first trying to win him an acquittal and, when that failed, appealing his case and protecting him from mistreatment in prison. Kohlman's idea was to show that what Sheila had done for Bailes was no more than what she did for every client. No romantic explanation was necessary; this was simply the bizarre way she practiced law. Miller, who was black, testified that when he lost his appeal, Sheila actually advised him to take his case to the NAACP and file a complaint against her as an ineffective counsel, which might lead to a reversal. He told of Sheila's intervention when he was ill in prison: "I was born with sickle-cell anemia, and it's a very serious disease, and I had took sick, and all they was giving me was Tylenol." After Sheila intervened, he received proper treatment. She visited him in prison, spoke with his prison counselor, arranged for his admission into disability and rehabilitation programs. Under Kohlman's questioning, Miller drew a portrait of Sheila as an angel of mercy, a sort of saint, who received no monetary award for her post-conviction efforts and who was utterly unlike any other court-appointed lawyer: "The rest of them, if I was getting locked up, they just wouldn't have nothing else to do with me." Miller's testimony might have impressed a New York jury; it evidently cut no ice with the all-white Alexandria jury.

As SHEILA and I approached her parents' house in the modest suburban neighborhood where she has lived all her life, she pointed out a few sights: Saint Rita's School, which she attended from the first to the eighth grade—a plain, low, red-brick building, erected in the early fifties—and, across the street from it, in the same unremarkable style, a three-story apartment building, wonderfully named Presidential Heights, where she lived as a small child, before her parents moved to their permanent home, on Holly Street, a few blocks away. Sheila parked the car at the rear of the Holly Street house and led me in through the front door. Within, all was in perfect order and a bit old-fashioned. Sheila's parents are in their mid-eighties, and although the house was built in the 1950s, its rooms are touched by a certain demurely feminine atmosphere connecting them to the 1940s. The living room is furnished with sofas and armchairs upholstered in ivory-white fabric; the floor is covered with two densely flowered Persian carpets; china figurines in period costumes are carefully arranged on shelves and tables; on the walls there is a miscellany of pictures: a pastel portrait of Sheila's late grandmother, done by a neighbor who signs her work "Babs"; a photograph of Sheila's great-grandfather as a baby; a watercolor of a resort in West Virginia where the family goes regularly on vacations; a Dürer print; a print of Ireland. On a side table stands a painted-wood sculpture of Saint Anthony of Padua with the infant Jesus in his arms. "As you know, Saint Anthony is the patron saint of lost objects," Sheila said. I didn't know, and she recited a verse she had learned as a child: "Dear Saint Anthony / Please come around / Something is lost / And cannot be found."

She looked around the room with quiet pleasure. "It's just a nice, comfortable living room in a nice, Colonial-style house. What else can I show you? This brass tray was brought back from Iraq twenty or thirty years ago by a friend of my parents. We had it made into a nice coffee table. And this is the chair where my dad sits. He likes to sit there in the evening with Dilsey on his lap, listening to his Lawrence Welk records." Dilsey is a rather disagreeable little dog, a Chihuahua, who barks at strangers and then trembles in remembered outrage when picked up by one of her masters.

Sheila led me to a finished basement, where she has an office and keeps the files of her case. To reach it, we passed through a dining room furnished with a cupboard of good china and decorative objects, and a large table with a lace tablecloth, and then through the kitchen. Kitchens, perhaps more fully than any other rooms, retain the flavor of their time. This one, with its breakfast counter, Hamilton Beach milkshake machine, lazy

Susan, its small cactuses in Mexican pottery on the windowsill over the sink, its linoleum of a certain light-green color, spoke unmistakably of the postwar period. Sheila's basement office, which also serves as her father's TV room, had walls of knotty pine, simple office furniture, and a well-worn armchair facing a small TV set. Sheila herself does not use the room very much these days. She no longer "works on the case." She has found paid work through an employment agency in Alexandria, which sends her out to jobs in the area as an office temporary. Only in the unlikely event that her conviction is overturned will she be able to practice law again (or to vote).

Dilsey, who had been sleeping in the father's armchair, expressed fury at my presence. When she subsided, Sheila went on with the story of what happened after she had risked her thousand dollars for Bailes. On the face of it, this was a really remarkable thing for her to have done. Bailes may not have been her type, but obviously something powerful wafted out toward her from this stranger to impel her rash generosity. "He looked sick, he had a bloated look." One of the unanswered questions about Bailes is whether he was ever as sick as he claimed to be or whether this was a part of the con. That he was a diabetic was beyond dispute. But the other afflictions he claimed in his various court appearances, appeals, and accusations against prison personnel were routinely dismissed by the authorities as devices. Sheila, in contrast, never wavered in her belief that Bailes's health was like Proust's and that his survival depended on constant special care and vigilance. Much of what she did seems lunatic for a lawyer to have done, but it begins to look less so when seen as a response to a health crisis. At their first meeting, in the Fairfax jail, Sheila had been persuaded that Bailes was in danger of losing his life if he stayed in prison much longer. This sense of crisis was the dominating feature of Sheila's four years of representing Bailes; it was what got her into the scalding water that kindly observers like Judge Turk tried to save her from. Whether Bailes was truly ill or a chronic faker is undeterminable—like practically everything else in his life. According to a birth certificate issued by the Commonwealth of Virginia, Bailes was born on June 5, 1940, in Lee County. But according to another certificate issued by the commonwealth, he was born on May 6, 1940. There is reason to suppose (though there is no proof) that the first document is genuine and the second one a forgery. In the infinite scheme of things, of course, it hardly matters whether Bailes was born one month later or earlier. But under the rigid anarchic principle by which his life was ruled, it was evidently necessary that even so immovable a fact as his date of birth be impossible to fix. For Bailes, the factual basis of life existed only as a kind of grid upon which to mount his design of defiant amorphousness. Just about every hard fact in Bailes's biography is eroded by an alternative contradictory fact (or two). Nothing about him can be pinned down.

A remarkable document entitled "Things That are Wrong and/or Incorrect in the West Virginia Presentence Report"—a list of sixty items compiled by Bailes—gives us a glimpse of the con artist at work on his subversive project. The West Virginia Presentence Report was prepared by a probation officer in 1979, on the occasion of Bailes's first major conviction, for giving false statements to a bank and for perjury. (There had been minor convictions for tax evasion and bad checks.) The "things wrong," according to Bailes's list, included the spelling of his name (the report gives it as Robert Eugene Bales, and he writes, "Name is incorrect—use Bobby Eugene Bailes—use the Bible record and the affidavit by my father"); the date of his mother's birth (the report gives it as March 15, 1918, and Bailes says it was March 15, 1908; however, both of Bailes's birth certificates give his mother's age as twenty-two in 1940); the number of his siblings (the report gives four; Bailes says six). Item 22 on Bailes's list is a correction of his father's name, and at this point, any lingering doubt the reader may have about Bailes's satiric intent is dispelled. The report gives the name as "James C.

Bales." This is wrong, Bailes writes. "My father's name is James Caleb Von Bailesious, shortened in 1939 to James Caleb Bailes. Then in 1943, they dropped the 'i' out of the name to keep from being recognized as a German Jew. Or this is what I was told." Item 23 goes on to say: "My mother's name was Juanita Rugh Maines, then changed to Robinette in 1933. Why? For some reason unknown because of the Germany Jew connection." Bailes went to prison for two years for the 1979 conviction, and he would be convicted and imprisoned three more times before his singular life was cut short, on September 20, 1995. He was out on parole and sitting on the sofa at his mother's house, watching TV with her, when he said he felt ill, and fell over dead.

Sheila's start with Bailes was astonishingly, and deceptively, auspicious. After freeing him with her thousand dollars, she argued his case before a magistrate in state court and succeeded in getting the charges against him—which again had to do with false information to a bank—dismissed "for lack of probable cause." The victory, however, was not only short-lived but the last victory Sheila ever enjoyed on Bailes's behalf. Two months later, in early May, he was arrested again, this time by federal agents, on the same charges, plus some new ones (a false Social Security number and false date of birth, among others), and was indicted in federal court. Sheila reluctantly agreed to represent him at trial. Her reluctance was based not on any premonition of personal disaster but on worry about her qualifications to argue a case in federal court; all her previous trial work had been in state courts. When she lost the case and Bailes went off to prison for five years, she blamed herself, and she continues to do so. "Where I blundered was to take on legal matters I wasn't prepared for," she said. "I should have just said no. It was an error of pride. I was flattered by Bobby's trust in me. But I didn't have the proper experience, and I didn't represent him adequately."

A few months after my visit to Sheila, I read a transcript of the trial (argued before a judge rather than a jury), and it was clear to me that Edward Bennett Williams himself could not have won an acquittal. Bailes had been indicted for lying to a bank in order to get a $12,500 loan: he had cited as collateral two automobiles he evidently didn't own, and he had submitted a false Social Security number, a false birth date, and a falsified tax return prepared by an accountant named Jo Ware, who evidently didn't exist (as I write "Jo Ware," I hear "Nowhere"). He had been arrested on the highway as he drove away from a hotel where he owed $522. Incriminating documents were found in his car, among them an identification card with Bailes's picture appearing above the name "Paul Price," and a packet of tax returns of past years, each page gleaming with Wite-Out. But even more eloquent than any documents was the testimony of the car itself. "In his automobile . . . were dirty clothing as well as dirty dishes, indicating when he is not in a hotel room, he is living out of his automobile," the government attorney said, arguing for high bail because of the probability of flight. A glimpse like this into Bailes's real life leaps out of the transcript, and it cannot have failed to fix itself in the mind of the judge deciding his fate. Dirty clothing and dirty dishes are no federal crime; but federal judges no less than juries form their impressions and act on them. In the Turk hearing, even if the verbatim record had not turned up and Sheila had been right in her legalism, she would not have prevailed, because Bailes was . . . what he was. He was a threat to society. At the sentencing hearing of the bank fraud and false Social Security number case, the government attorney, Bud Albright, arguing for a stiff sentence, spoke of "the victims that he has left in his wake" and went on:

Your Honor, I don't think there is any way we are going to reform this man. He has had a chance to be reformed.

He has had—I forget the number of arrests—I think seven or eight convictions. He has been convicted of perjury. He has been convicted of bank fraud before. He has been sentenced to 12 years in jail. Nothing seems to do him any good. . . .

Albright's speech then took a curious turn:

I was sitting this morning in my office, and I had with me the state registrar, Mr. Booker, whose office was a victim of Mr. Bailes in the birth certificate situation. He told me he spent over 100 hours trying to sort out the mess that Mr. Bailes had caused. And he asked me a question, and he said . . . "Why is this man on the street? Why is he still out there?" . . . And frankly, Your Honor, I couldn't answer him, except to say that the system does not protect the public very well from people like that.

Like the dirty clothing and dirty dishes, the mess Bailes created in the registrar's office was not the crime he was indicted for. But it was the crime he was convicted of. Mr. Booker's cry from the heart about his one hundred wasted hours is only one among the many moans and whimpers that echo through the chronicles of Bailes's passage through the courts. Bailes's real threat to the public was not the various petty chicaneries he committed in order to eat and to pay for gas but the great disorder he generated, as if by an ineluctable inner compulsion, wherever he set foot. The unregulated insurance companies were the emblem of Bailes's own defining unruliness. Chaos was the medium in which he could breathe; order suffocated him. "It's been an unusually garbled trial, I guess you could say," the exhausted judge who presided over Bailes's 1988 "scheme to defraud" trial in Charlotte said during his charge to the jury. "In fact, I guess it's the worst I've ever had." Bailes acted as his own attorney in that trial, which was indeed garbled but whose outcome was never in question. If Sheila's criminal trial was a duel, Bailes's trial in Charlotte was a bear-baiting. The government had him cornered; the dogs toyed with him, moved in on him, and efficiently killed him. But such was Bailes's genius for creating confusion that it had taken the government nearly four years to prepare its case; more than fifty witnesses took the stand to testify about the workings of his insurance scam. Similarly, it has taken me over a year to grasp that Sheila, his partner in the crime of getting things hopelessly balled up, stands, in her strange and pitiful way, for something rather magnificent. Her inability to see what was staring everybody else in the face about Bailes, her refusal to label him a con man and write him off, her insistence that his pleadings not be automatically dismissed as frivolous because they came from him—are the signs not of naïveté, as some observers have believed them to be, but of a bracing idealism. She once said to me, "If it's not respectable and safe for a lawyer to represent someone whom the government brands as a bad person, an enemy of the state, then we're moving up the continuum toward a system they have in many countries—not only China—where a person accused of a crime is represented by an employee of the state, who is expected to make certain very narrow defenses, sometimes limited to 'mitigating circumstances,' in the course of negotiating a plea agreement. That's not been our tradition in the United States."

This is a cliché, of course, one regularly mouthed by criminal defense lawyers when called upon to justify their representation of a noxious client—a Claus von Bülow or an O. J. Simpson or a Joel Steinberg. But Sheila's willingness to test the system and stay the course with a Bob Bailes is something different. She gained nothing in money or publicity: this was not a glamorously or chillingly evil man; nor did the case have any political or social significance, or even entertainment value. The work Sheila did for Bailes, in fact, seemed so not worth doing, so pointless and thankless, that only romance could explain her motives. Her retort—that she was doing it because it was her task as a lawyer—seemed too strange to credit. Her continued respectfulness and loyalty toward Bailes seems similarly remarkable. ("Sheila, how can you call him a businessman when you *know* he was a crook?" I have shrilled at her.) But when you stop and think about what a lawyer's obligations to his client are, you realize that Sheila is simply fulfilling them to the letter: Lawyers are not supposed to bad-mouth their clients. In fact, they're not supposed to talk about them to outsiders at all; and Sheila wrote to me only because Bailes's death had freed her of her obligation of silence. But nothing, evidently, will ever free her of her lawyer's habit of presenting a client in the best possible light. In death as in life, he remains a client. In contrast, the lawyers I spoke to who had represented the various subsidiary rascals of this history—the lawyers of Manfredi, Morris, and Zinke, for example—greeted my opening mention of their former clients with a knowing little laugh, as Sheila's own lawyers in varying degrees betrayed her. Even the punctilious Abrams permitted himself a mild disparagement: "Have you ever eaten with Sheila? She sent back the coffee three times."

DILSEY WAS roused again—this time by the sound of the elder McGoughs' car in the driveway. Sheila took me upstairs to meet her parents. Irene McGough was tiny and peppy and chatty and refined. She had the exaggerated freshness—like an overcleaned painting—that is a characteristic of many elderly American women. Her white hair was arranged in careful curls around her head, and she wore slacks and a daintily embroidered blouse. Behind her silver-rimmed glasses, her blue eyes, the color of forget-me-nots, watered slightly and becomingly. Thomas McGough, a retired medical doctor, called "Doc" by Irene, was short and round and courteous and melancholy. Instead of a tie, he wore a Mexican bolo, which he had done, he later told me, ever since a Mexican friend, twenty years earlier, took one off his own neck and, in an obligatory impulsive gesture, gave it to him when he had admired it. This independence of costume on the part of an elderly, in every other respect conventional, suburban doctor made a strong impression on me, and I tried to find out more about it, but he had no explanation except that he liked his bolo.

The McGoughs had ash marks on their foreheads, and Irene asked me if I would stay for a dinner of Lenten tuna casserole, which she had prepared in the morning. I accepted, and Irene went off to the kitchen to prepare vegetables; she wouldn't hear of my helping her. "No, she really doesn't want you to," Sheila said when I looked questioningly at her. The mother was the power of the family, and Sheila was the subdued, obedient child. The kitchen was the mother's domain; after dinner, Sheila would be allowed to do the dishes. At table, Irene rattled on as Sheila and I put in an occasional word; Tom McGough didn't speak at all. Once he had said grace—a not perfunctory one—he subsided into the traditional role of the silent man in a house of chattering women. During one of Irene's longer passages, I glanced over at Sheila and saw her looking at her mother with an expression of rapt love I've never forgotten. I don't remember what Irene was saying, and I'm not even sure that Sheila was listening to her; she was simply loving her. As if by preagreement (I later learned that there had actually been one), nothing was said about Sheila's case. The table talk was domestic, feminine, friendly—and I fell easily into my role of the nice friend Sheila had brought home from school to meet her mom and dad. Irene's chatter was pleasant and undemanding, Tom's silence was unthreatening, and the tuna casserole was incomparable.

WHEN, A few days after my return to New York, I telephoned Kirkpatrick MacDonald, it was like accidentally disturbing a hornet's nest. On hearing the name Sheila McGough, Mac-Donald flew into a rage. "Why are you writing about her?" he asked. "This is a woman who has done terrible things. It took me a long time to put her out of business. I had to badger the government into prosecuting her. She is an unprincipled person. I have lost enormous amounts of money because of her and because of that crook Bob Bailes. I hope he stays in jail forever." I told MacDonald that Bailes was dead. "Good!" MacDonald said. "I'm very pleased to hear it!" Then he said, "I am a public figure. I don't want anything to appear in print about me that won't contribute to my good reputation. I will cooperate with you only if I know that your story won't be slanted the wrong way." I said that my story probably *would* be slanted the wrong way, and prepared to hang up. But MacDonald kept me on the line, and a few days later I was ringing the doorbell of the brownstone on West Seventy-eighth Street where he conducts his investment banking business and also lives. The large carved wood door was opened by a slight man with sandy, thinning hair, wearing a tweed jacket and corduroys, and exuding a genial, almost professorial air. All traces of the irascible man on the telephone were gone. He led me into an elegant front parlor with high ceilings and ornate moldings, furnished with antique furniture and rugs, and motioned me to a small sofa covered with yellow silk brocade.

In answer to my questions, MacDonald drew an outline of his life that offered few clues to the mystery of his vindictiveness toward Sheila. "I come from a wealthy family in San Francisco," he began, and went on to speak of his studies at Yale, Oxford, and the University of Geneva, where he started to work for a doctorate in political economics but didn't finish a dissertation entitled "The Chilinization of Copper." As he talked, MacDonald punctuated his words with a complicitous little grimace—a shrug and a turning down of the mouth—as if to draw me into his own skeptical and amused view of life. "If I had finished my thesis and gotten my Ph.D., I would have been unbearably intellectual," he said, making the grimace. He came to New York and worked in various venerable financial institutions, such as Lehman Brothers and Morgan Guaranty. Then he joined the militaristic encounter group est, which "changed my way of looking at things" and emboldened him to go into business for himself as a private investment banker. The business prospered. It was conducted, he said, "on a high level of international finance, for which I had a great knack." He and his first wife were divorced in the mid-eighties, and he has since remarried; he has two grown children from the first marriage. He belongs to the Knickerbocker Club in New York and the Bohemian Club in San Francisco.

Turning to the transaction that had brought Bailes and Sheila and the FBI and Hulkower, and now me, into his life, MacDonald said it was his trust of Zinke that had determined his action. "At that period in my business career, I was willing to trust anyone who had a good background, been to good schools, worked for the right company. I knew Philip socially, and I trusted him. He was going to put up half the money, and when he didn't put up his half, I said I would be happy to put it up for him. 'You'll owe me the money,' I said. 'You're my friend.' "

MacDonald now knows that Zinke is not such an upstanding citizen—that he has been convicted of stealing five million dollars from his partners in a business called Stonehenge Investment Notes 1, Ltd. (The conviction was reversed by the New York State Court of Appeals on the Gilbertian ground that since Zinke was a partner in the firm, he had stolen money from himself, and stealing money from yourself is no crime.) In 1993, the wily Zinke again escaped imprisonment by snitching on Norman Lida, a lawyer who had been engaged with him in an inventive money-laundering scheme that allowed clients of a prostitution ring to pay with American Express cards by disguising the charges for sex as charges for limousine service. By this time, as it happens, Zinke was no longer Zinke. In 1991, he had legally changed his name to Philip Schuyler, Count Von Preysing. As a reward for his testimony against Lida, Zinke—or "Mr. Von Preysing," as the republican prosecutor called him at the trial—was sentenced to five years probation. MacDonald told me that he had a judgment against Zinke for the $37,500 he had loaned him, and expects to collect on it, although he doesn't know where Zinke is. "I'll find Zinke," he said. "Remember, this is a man I used to have dinner with on Central Park West. He'll show up, and because he's basically a gentleman, if he has any money, he'll pay."

MacDonald's comments about Manfredi and Boccagna were less respectful. He spoke of Manfredi as a "small-time crook, an intermediary, a marginal guy." "People on Long Island do all kinds of funny things," he said. "Boccagna was young and scared. He knew he was caught up in something that wasn't legal. I said to him at his deposition, 'You keep your nose clean. If we decide to go after you, you're dead meat.' Alan Morris was highly cooperative. If he hadn't been cooperative, I would have sued him. I would have sued Manfredi, Boccagna, and Morris. They were in the chain of fraud."

MacDonald's explanation for his hounding of Sheila came at the end of the interview. It took the form of a very long story concerning a crooked developer in Washington, D.C., to whom some European investors had foolishly entrusted several million dollars for a housing development. MacDonald was called in to investigate a sudden mystifying shortage of funds and discovered that the developer, a Mr. H., had siphoned off two million dollars for himself. He confronted Mr. H. "Mr. H. looked at me and said, 'I took my profits a little early.' So I said, 'You could go to jail for this. You had better cooperate with me. I won't say anything to the authorities, and in return you will give me everything else you have.' So he gave me a large piece of land out in Maryland, right next to where they were in the process of building the last metro station in Washington—the Shady Grove station. I took the land and developed it, and I recovered the two million dollars that those European investors had lost, and made myself a very large fee for my efforts. I didn't denounce Mr. H. Then I got a call from someone who had seen me working on the development in Maryland, and he said, 'Isn't that interesting—after giving you that property, Mr. H. went out and raised five million dollars from two other groups, and stole all their money, too. They've spent a quarter million in legal fees, trying to catch up with him. If you had denounced him, he might not have been able to do that.' So I said to myself, 'If I'm ever again involved with anybody who flagrantly breaks the law, I will do my civic duty and at least put the public on notice that it's dealing with a crook.' And that's the reason why, when Sheila McGough settled with me, I said, 'Wait a minute. Citizen's obligation here. If I don't put her out of business, somebody can come to me and say, "You knew this lady was a crook, and you helped yourself to her Errors and Omissions insurance, and you didn't say anything to anybody. What kind of a citizen are you?" ' In my suit against her, on the advice of counsel, I made a strategic decision not to accuse her of any criminal activity, because her Errors and Omissions insurance would not have paid if I had won a judgment for fraud. So I just said I wanted the escrow money back. When I got it, and she didn't close up her briefcase and go home, I said, 'Well, I've got to get her briefcase closed.' "

WHEN I telephoned Mark Hulkower, he, too, spoke about the "slant" of my story, but his tone was quite different from MacDonald's. It was good-humored, even a little humorous, and he was under no illusion about which way my narrative would go. He knew full well that journalists don't write stories celebrating just convictions, that journalism's reflex is to disturb, not to pat down, the soil. But he felt it was a mistake for prosecutors to refuse to speak to journalists and so ensure their hostility. "I don't want my young son to read about me as a meanie," he said. "I will be glad to speak to you and defend my side of the case."

A few weeks later, I arrived at Hulkower's office, in a large law firm on Connecticut Avenue. Hulkower had recently left the Justice Department to enter private practice; his work now was all in criminal defense. He received me in a luxurious conference room of a kind of neo-classical character, whose sea-green walls matched the sea in the nautical paintings on them, and whose glass-top conference table evoked one of those absurdly long limousines one sees in New York at night; fifty people could have sat at it. Hulkower is youngish, of middle size, with an assertive stride and a searching gaze. Almost immediately, the adversarial relationship that he had been at such pains to avoid on the telephone developed between us, precipitated by my gesture of placing a tape recorder on the table. He said that he wanted what he said to be treated as "background" rather than as words for quotation. It later struck me that what Hulkower was proposing was the journalistic equivalent of an escrow agreement. His words would be at no risk: they would be deposited in the safe place of "background," where nothing could come of them. The dangerous terrain of print, where words count, where they have consequences, is skirted by the interviewee who speaks for "background" only. Hulkower wanted my sympathetic ear, but he didn't want to pay for it in the nonrefundable currency of quotation.

When I declined the escrow deal, Hulkower said, "Very well. But I will be very constrained in what I say," and proceeded to answer my questions as tersely and uncommunicatively as possible, as if miming the word "inhibition" in a charade. However, he couldn't sustain the charade for long and presently returned to his normal vigorous and incisive, fluent and animated speech.

Of all the people in this story, Hulkower is the one most familiar and, in a sense, congenial to me. He grew up in New York, where I grew up, in a liberal Jewish family like mine (his parents were active in the labor movement), and I feel I understand him as I will never understand MacDonald—or, if it comes to that, Sheila—and that if we had met in another context there would be much common ground between us. But in the context of this narrative, there is an electric fence between us. If Sheila is my heroine, Hulkower has to be my villain. A journalistic narrative is a kind of lumbering prehistoric beast that knocks over everything in its path as it makes its way through the ancient forest of basic plots. My sneaking liking for Hulkower simply has no place in my story. My assumption that Hulkower is a decent and well-meaning man must be held up to the strictest scrutiny; I must search his words and writings for signs of bad faith.

During our talk, I asked him a question raised in one of Stuart Abrams's appeal briefs—from which he gathered that I had not read his own reply brief—and he said mockingly, "It's interesting that they only gave you their own brief." But it's not interesting, it's obvious; we all believe that our side of the story is the only story. Sheila's feelings about Hulkower are unambivalent: She hates his guts. When I proposed to her that it was MacDonald who was responsible for her ruin—that it was he who had vengefully set in motion the events that led to her conviction and imprisonment and that Hulkower was just doing his job—she waved the idea away. In her view, MacDonald was a mere instrument of the all-powerful and ruthless government authorities who had "targeted" her and Bailes. Her undying hatred is reserved for Hulkower, along with Henry Hudson, his chief in the Justice Department; for an FBI agent named Bob Carroll; and for "Buddy" Albright and Debra Stuart, two government attorneys who prosecuted Bailes. Toward MacDonald and Manfredi and Morris and other of the government witnesses who helped to convict her, Sheila can feel nothing but a kind of benign contempt. We pick our enemies as we pick our friends. We have a taste in enemies. Sheila's taste runs to "corrupt government officials." The idea of them stirs her imagination. MacDonald and Manfredi and the others aren't real to her. They have never become characters in her inner drama.

At the long conference table, Hulkower ridiculed the idea that he was "out to get" Sheila McGough. "I didn't know her," he said. "I had no animus toward her. I joined the U.S. Attorney's Office in 1989, and this was one of the cases I was given. She claims there was a vendetta against her. But then why did they give the case to someone who had never heard of her and who was new and green?" In an appeal brief of 1992, Stuart Abrams raised the question of why the government had "decided to take a civil dispute that had been settled three years earlier and convert it into this criminal case." I asked Hulkower this question now, and he replied, "A lawyer is convicted of fourteen fraud crimes, and you ask me why the case was brought? The jury found evidence beyond a reasonable doubt—and the district appeals court confirmed their verdict—that she had defrauded people, that she had lied, that she had committed perjury, and that she had obstructed justice. It's obvious why the case was brought." He paused and said, "The better question is: Why would they think that she should be allowed to engage in that kind of conduct simply because she is a lawyer?"

THE UNCONSCIOUS, which often awes us with its subtlety, can also paint in rather garish colors, as mine did when it arranged that after my visit to the Catholic McGoughs' on Ash Wednesday I should "accidentally" next visit them on Easter weekend; it is thus that life imitates kitsch. Sheila once again insisted on meeting my noon train, and again, when we arrived at the house on Holly Street, the parents were away. We talked at the kitchen table this time, leaving the downstairs office to Dilsey; but it wasn't until two-thirty that Sheila suddenly remembered that she ought to have offered me lunch. Although she has lived in the house since the age of seven (with two interruptions: the first to live in an apartment in Georgetown with a classmate from college shortly after graduation, and the second to go to prison), she moved around the kitchen as if she had never seen it before, making tentative, mystified motions and peering into cupboards with a vague and wondering look, as she brought out some bread and cookies and fruit. She ate almost nothing herself. Her mind was on the case, on the task of giving me the most truthful and complete answers to the questions I asked—answers that made me want to put my hands over my ears and that frequently caused me to impatiently interrupt her. I kept trying to keep her to the point (my point), and she would meekly subside, like a dog accepting a scolding for something it knows it hasn't done, puzzled but uncomplaining. Why, I pressed her, if she was Bailes's criminal lawyer, had she got involved in his business affairs?

"Why not?" she said. "A criminal defendant has the right to buy a house, sue somebody, go into personal bankruptcy, pursue any number of things in civil court. Just because he's under indictment doesn't mean that all his civil rights are gone."

But didn't the insurance company deal arouse some suspicion in her? Didn't it seem a little fishy?

"No, it didn't seem fishy. It didn't seem like anything odd or strange or something I should be wary of. It wasn't something that I gave a lot of time or thought to. When I permitted Bobby to have the buyers send the down payment to my client trust account, it was an accommodation."

I said, "Tell me this: If you had thought the charters were phony, that this was a scam, would you still have 'accommodated' Bobby and allowed the money to come into your trust account?"

"That's a fair question," Sheila said. "No. I certainly wouldn't have."

"So, conversely, you thought it was legitimate."

"I had no reason to believe it wasn't."

"But Bailes already had a record. He'd been in prison."

"Yes, Bobby had taken some falls. But if you look at the charges, they weren't very much. One of them was tax evasion: failure to pay all his proper taxes. Yes, that certainly is a crime. I don't want to diminish it. But I think that few Americans believe that someone who doesn't pay all his owed taxes is the worst sort of vicious criminal, who ought never to be allowed back into society. Bobby was also convicted of misstating, inflating, and inaccurately describing assets as collateral for loans. Again, that certainly is a crime if true—an antisocial act—but not the sort of thing that most people would consider the indication of a truly depraved mind and of someone who ought never to be treated as a decent human being."

A few weeks earlier, Sheila had sent me, among other items, an article about her case by a journalist named Amanda Spake, which appeared in the *Washington Post Magazine* in July 1991. I had been struck by something Sheila had told Spake: "I have an extremely close relationship with my blood kin, but I don't really have close friends." I now asked her if she could tell me something more about this tendency to keep people outside the family at a distance.

"Yes, it's true," Sheila said, "but it never seemed to be a disability at work. When I was sixteen, I got my work permit and got a summer job at the Pentagon as a clerk-typist. I worked for a couple of lieutenant colonels and did a good job. They gave me a little party at the end of the summer, and they spoke so highly of me that the next summer the head of the personnel office grabbed me as a junior secretary fill-in for the World Bank. Then, when I graduated from college, I was immediately hired by a prestigious scientific institute, the Carnegie Institute, and I did well enough in the publications office that when my supervisor left she recommended me to take her place. In this job, I dealt not only with administrative people at Carnegie but with world-class scientists; I was responsible for editing the copy of these very eminent people. Sometimes I would even make suggestions for rewording their copy. Apparently I interacted well enough with all these people that for nineteen years I got one promotion after another, until I hit the natural ceiling, which was to be the head of the publications department."

When Sheila began to speak of the next stage in her career and of her excellent "interactions" with legal clients, I could contain my impatience no longer and interrupted to say that I had never doubted her social adroitness and that my question had simply been an attempt to know her better, to understand what it felt like to be so much more comfortable with family than with people outside it. Later, I realized that Sheila had answered my question. She had enacted the phenomenon I was investigating. She wouldn't engage with me—wouldn't tell me the intimate secret I was trying to pry from her—for had she done so, she would have belied her statement "I don't really have close friends." The currency of friendship is privileged information: confidences, confessions, self-revelations. But Sheila doesn't trade in this currency with outsiders, possibly not even with blood kin. By answering my question with a long, dull history of her professional successes, she was telling me (as she had been telling me all along) that she wanted our relationship to remain strictly, dully professional.

I asked her why she had moved back home after living in Georgetown on her own. "For a while I needed to have my own place," she replied. "I thought it important for me not to just go on living in my childhood home. But then I decided that was silly. Why should I pay rent every month when I had my mom and dad, who wanted me at home? They were a lot of fun—I just enjoyed them so much. So I went back. It wasn't the money. I was already getting little raises at Carnegie. I had made the point that, yes, I was a big girl, I could live on my own and take out my trash every week and scrub my kitchen floor."

"Was there something that precipitated your decision to go back?"

"No, not that I remember. My mother probably said, 'Now you've made your point. Why don't you come back and enjoy life and save your money?' "

Dilsey, once again roused to hysteria by the sound of a car in the driveway, appeared in the kitchen to greet the older McGoughs, who were back from a trip to Irene's hairdresser. Tom picked up the dog and carried her to the living room. Irene took in the kitchen-table still life of bread and cookies that had been unceremoniously dumped there in their wrappings, rather than nicely set out on plates, and voiced a mother's displeasure. Sheila took no umbrage, put the offending objects away, and complimented Irene on her hairdo. A change had taken place in the household between my two visits. A few weeks earlier, Irene had undergone a cataract operation, and it had gone awry—had left her with worse, rather than better, vision. Now underneath the chatter and perkiness and bossiness there was fear, and also anger at the "top" Johns Hopkins surgeon who had done this to her. She was unable to read or drive, and was forced to accept help that she would ordinarily have indignantly spurned. The drama had begun which few families with elders in their eighties escape, and which sets in motion an unexpected and unwelcome reshuffling of roles. The seniors, who were supporting players for the young stars for as long as anyone can remember, are suddenly thrust onto center stage, their hip fractures, heart stoppages, cancers, emphysemas, dementias providing the données for painful plots set in medical examining rooms, hospital emergency rooms, intensive care units, nursing homes, and hospices. Sheila's drama of trial and conviction and prison had paled—as all dramas of middle-aged children with aging parents pale—in the lurid light of the parents' last turn.

A little discussion ensued about the preparation of dinner. Under the new dispensation, Sheila was allowed in the kitchen to help with cooking; the question was what to do with the visiting writer. Perhaps I'd like to go watch the news with Tom in the living room? I said I would prefer to chop vegetables in the kitchen. Sheila then asked me a question that I have never forgotten—not because what she asked was so remarkable but because she had asked it: until that moment, she had never asked me (and would never again ask me) a question about myself. In her puristic idea of the journalistic encounter, it was not the subject's place to question the journalist. But something about the image of me chopping vegetables so disturbed her notion of the writer as someone who only writes that she blurted out: "Oh, you know how to cook?" When I said I did, Irene loyally put in, "Sheila is a very good cook," to which Sheila said, "No, I'm not. I don't know how to do it."

There turned out to be no vegetables to chop; this had been done in the morning by mother and daughter. Salmon, asparagus, cauliflower, and potatoes—all prepared for cooking—were produced from the refrigerator. While I boiled the vegetables and Irene broiled the fish, Sheila made a hollandaise sauce from a prepared mix. Wincing inwardly, I watched her empty the packet of white powder into a saucepan of cold milk and stir it in a vague way over a low flame. All my cooking experience told me that she should have either stirred the milk, a little at a time, into the powder or have brought the milk to a boil before combining it with the powder. I covertly glanced at the instructions on the empty packet. "Mix the milk and the powder, and cook over low heat while stirring," it said. A few minutes later, Irene looked over at Sheila and voiced the same concern. "Dear, shouldn't you have boiled the milk first?" As Sheila looked meekly at her mother, I was able to come to her defense and report that she had followed the instructions to the letter. ("We may not like the rule, but it's very clear.")

After dinner, by prearrangement, I interviewed Irene in the living room, while Sheila did the dishes and Tom retired to the downstairs study. My proposal that we postpone the interview until her eye was better was dismissed, and as soon as I had turned on the tape recorder she began a speech she had evidently prepared for the occasion:

"I have the greatest love and respect for my country, but I have become disillusioned with the government. I have come to believe that some of us are too naive. We feel that our country will never do anything bad, that the other countries have their Gestapo and KGB but that we are just wonderful. I now believe that our Justice Department is an American KGB. I have no respect for the Justice Department. Sheila's case turned me completely against it. My husband and I spent thousands of dollars printing up briefs and walking the halls of Congress hand-delivering them to senators and congressmen. But when you're nobody, like me, you get the brush-off. When you're just an older, middle-class taxpayer, forget it. If you're prominent, if you have a lot of money—well, it may make a difference. I have become so disillusioned, I don't even talk about it anymore. We worked so hard. We contacted so many people."

"What had you felt during Sheila's trial?" I asked.

"My first feeling was one of disbelief that this could be happening. I couldn't believe what I was seeing and hearing. My son had some problems in the sixties. He was a flower child. Now he's very ordinary, down-to-earth. But Sheila? Sheila was very quiet, very reserved. Lots of friends. No. She was very popular, but no intimates. She was very popular with men, she had lots of dates, I never worried about that. No problems until this happened. Recently her social life has been very quiet. But then there were absolutely no problems. In any job there can be little jealousies—say, if you get promoted ahead of somebody else. But that was it. To me—let me emphasize this—there never was a color problem. I was born and raised in Baltimore. Our family always had black help, and when I got married and moved around the country with Doc, I always had black help. I had black help here in Alexandria: I had Canary Smith. Canary was with us for years—an elderly black woman who took charge. I could go out for a day and she took care of the kids, she took care of everything. I never had a problem. When I was growing up, I was seven years old before I knew there was a difference, a difference in skin. So I can say that my children never had any problems with race—never, never, never. I don't think this entered the trial. I don't think so."

"Then what made you think of it just now?" I asked about her arresting non sequitur.

"I just—I don't know," Irene said. My question discomposed her. "There have been so many things thrown in," she added uncertainly. "I just wonder whether this isn't something else they would say."

What exactly caused the "color problem" to float into Irene's mind, as she spoke about Sheila's old problem-free life, never emerged; but her remark about "so many things thrown in" was well taken. In building its case against Sheila, the government had gone to extraordinary lengths to present her as a woman who could do no right; racism would have been just another of her vilenesses. Over fifty people were subpoenaed to testify against her. It was like one of those nightmares of guilt, where everyone you have ever known has gathered to accuse you of wrongdoing. People Sheila had no reason to think of as enemies—to think of at all, in fact—appeared for the government and showed themselves to be no friends. One of these was a woman named Linda Cooley, who had been a receptionist and notary public for the suite of offices where Sheila had her law practice and who had darkly watched Sheila during the period she was preparing her defense of Bailes against the bank fraud and false Social Security number charges and, later, when she was receiving collect calls from him in prison. Cooley's contribution to the government's narrative was twofold. In the first segment of her testimony, playing the role of the disapproving servant piously reporting the irregularities she has observed, she fleshed out the narrative of the romantic attachment between Sheila and Bailes. She told of the roses that had been delivered to the suite, addressed to one Agnes Thunderbird, who turned out to be Sheila, and had come with a card that said, "Love, Bob." (Sheila told me that her middle name is Agnes but she does not know what Bailes meant by Thunderbird—she never thought to ask him.) She reported on the girlish flutter produced in Sheila whenever Bailes called and on Sheila's displays of anger when she missed a call from him because no one had gone to fetch her in the ladies' room. "Did there come a time," the junior prosecutor, David Barger, prompted Cooley, "that she appeared to take more interest in her appearance?"

"It seemed that way, yes," Cooley replied.

" . . . And so, because of that, on occasion, would she be in the rest room when she would receive calls from Mr. Bailes?" Barger asked, making a bad mistake, which Kohlman exploited in his cross-examination.

"Now, you pride yourself on your appearance, don't you?" Kohlman asked Cooley.

A: Yes.

Q: You take time to, as men and women do, to kind of dress up a little bit, right?

A: Yes.

Q: Do you ever dress up, Ms. Cooley, so that you can talk to someone on the telephone?

A: I don't understand.

Q: Well, I don't either.

Examples like these of Kohlman's quickness and sharpness as a cross-examiner gleam out of the trial transcript; but they also illustrate the futility of even the most brilliant defense play in a game already lost. In the face of the opposition's saturation bombing—of Hulkower's devastating opening address, with its narrative of reckless "misconduct," and his relentless parade of witnesses testifying to Sheila's misdeeds—Kohlman's rapier thrusts counted for little indeed. The second part of Cooley's testimony, even more than the first, struck a terrible blow to the defense. What made it so damaging was its relationship to the testimony of the previous witness, a man named Mack Cain, who had worked as a paralegal for S. S. Smith in Abingdon. Cain had told a damning story about Sheila's attempt to get him to falsely notarize two documents called "superseding contracts" on the night before MacDonald's lawsuit was to be tried. Now Linda Cooley testified that she, too, had been asked by Sheila to notarize a document that had not been signed in her presence. Actually, the two incidents were very different. But going by fast, as trial testimony does, they seemed (as Hulkower intended them to seem) like two instances of the same "pattern of deceit." Any doubts the jury might have had about Cain's story were put to rest when Linda Cooley got up and said that, in effect, the same thing had happened to her.

Sheila has told me that Mack Cain's testimony about the "superseding contracts" was untrue—was simply invented— and she is corroborated by Kenneth Labowitz, a lawyer who had represented her in the MacDonald suit and who testified on the fourth day of her criminal trial. By that time, however, the narrative of the superseding contracts was such a solid and well-crafted structure, one whose joints had such a nice fit, that it couldn't be shaken. The narrative was introduced by a yet earlier witness, Michael Wyatt, MacDonald's lawyer in his suit against Sheila. If some of Hulkower's witnesses—Manfredi, for example—required careful handling lest they blow up under cross-examination, Wyatt was quite beyond a prosecutor's dream of impregnable respectability. (Q: How are you employed, Mr. Wyatt? A: I am in the federal government. Q: What do you do? A: I am the associate deputy secretary of labor.) Wyatt's storytelling powers, moreover, were on Hulkower's own level of excellence. Under the prosecutor's questioning, Wyatt told of how, a week or ten days before the

MacDonald suit was to go to trial, Sheila's defense suddenly produced two contracts, both signed by Bailes and Manfredi, that superseded all previous contracts in the transaction. "They would have practically destroyed our lawsuit," Wyatt declared. They "defined the deposit as a nonrefundable deposit rather than an escrow payment." Wyatt continued, "We had picked through a mountain of documents at great length, and analyzed and reanalyzed all the details. We had depositions. We had gone through numerous hearings in this Court on motions, and to find, this late in the case, two documents that nobody [had] referred to, never mentioned, never hinted at existing, suddenly these documents, which provide defenses, show up. . . . I was absolutely stunned."

Q: Other than that, was there anything about those documents that caught your attention?

A: Well, as a matter of fact, the one I remember is [Exhibit] Number 25, because when I saw the signature that purported to be the signature of Mr. Manfredi, it's just one of these things, I knew I had seen that somewhere before. . . . I got in my car and absolutely raced back to my office over in the District, where I had my box of documents, and I pawed through the box and found the signature. I knew I had seen it.

Q: What do you mean—

A: There was just something funny about it.

What was funny was that Manfredi's signature on the superseding contracts was an exact duplicate of his signature on the document Wyatt found in his box. Signatures, as we know, are never exactly the same; there is always some slight variation.

"Is it fair to say that it was your conclusion that that signature of Frank Manfredi had been lifted from another document?" Hulkower asked.

"That was certainly what we concluded," Wyatt replied.

Who did the lifting of Manfredi's signature from one document to another was never established at trial, though the project bears an unmistakable Bailesian touch. The fact that Bailes was in prison at the time of the MacDonald suit would hardly have foreclosed the possibility that he was the author of the forgery. Bailes generated as much paperwork from his cell as most lawyers and businessmen generate from their offices. He sued almost every judge, prosecutor, and lawyer who came his way—sometimes calling on Sheila for assistance in the filing of the suit and sometimes filing on his own—and he continued to pursue his various remarkable business ventures. When I asked Sheila how the superseding contracts had come into the Mac-Donald suit, she replied, "I first heard about them from Bobby. I was talking to him on the telephone every day then, and one day he said something about some stuff Mack Cain would be sending from Abingdon, copies of some contracts. The stuff arrived and I made copies—or maybe Ken Labowitz made copies of the copies; I no longer remember who—and we sent them to Wyatt and also filed them with the court."

"Do you think it is possible that Bailes, or perhaps Cain working under Bailes's direction, could have cooked up those contracts?" I said. Sheila reluctantly said yes. It appeared that Cain and Bailes had renewed an acquaintance going back to the seventies in 1985, when S. S. Smith was representing Bailes in various messy noncriminal matters and Bailes had inserted himself into Smith's office as he would insert himself into Sheila's the following year. Before long, Cain was supplementing his paralegal's salary by working for Bailes and, after that, for a man named Al Johnson, to whom Bailes had actually succeeded in selling one of the insurance companies. (Johnson, who lived in Florida, spent two years operating the company and battling state commissioners who would not recognize his right to sell unregulated insurance; he finally gave up and joined the club of Bailes's "victims." Sheila holds up the Johnson purchase as evidence that the insurance charters were not a one-hundred-percent certain fraud, and points to the fact that Hulkower didn't call Johnson as a witness at her trial as a further sign of his bad faith.)

Although Wyatt's testimony about the superseding documents clearly demonstrated their fakeness, it didn't implicate Sheila in their manufacture. This was left to Mack Cain, who, as it seemed, could scarcely contain his pleasure at the chance to contribute to Hulkower's narrative of the evil woman. Cain testified that he had been subpoenaed to appear as a defense witness at the MacDonald trial but had no idea why, since he knew nothing about the transaction in dispute. Sheila, he said, arranged for him to fly first class from Abingdon to Washington and to be put up in a suite at a hotel in Alexandria. When he arrived and called Sheila in her office to find out "what this was all about," she said that "the walls have 'ears'" and that she would come over to his hotel room. Cain went on to speak of his disinclination, as "somebody who is married and got three children," to meet with Sheila in a hotel room. But Sheila prevailed, he said, and she came to the suite.

Hulkower prompted him: "Tell us what happened when she came by. Was there some small talk or anything like that?"

A: Chitchat, you know—how's the kids? how's the wife? how's the job? are you enjoying what you are doing?—and you know, kind of put me on my guard right then and there.

Q: Why did that put you on guard?

A: Well, I had three children, and when my children come up to me and say, "I love you, Daddy," and kiss me on the cheek, I look at them and say, "What do you want?" And you know, here, now, this chitchat, and you know I was just, down inside, you know, trying to say, you know, I just had this feeling like, "What do you want?"

Q: Now, in the conversation, did Ms. McGough tell you how her civil case was going?

A: Said it wasn't going good at all. She said she was unhappy with the way it was going. It was just going downhill.

Q: After that, did she ask you to do something for her?

A: Yes. She presented two documents to me and asked if I had seen them before. I said no. She—I glanced at the first part of it, the superseding contracts, glanced over it, and it had a signature that was purportedly to be Bob Bailes, and one purported to be Mr. Manfredi.

Q: And did Ms. McGough ask you to do anything to those contracts, those superseding contracts?

A: She asked if I would notarize them as if I was present when they were signed.

Q: And did she ask you to do anything in regards to your testimony at trial the next day?

A: If I would have gone and done that, for me to testify that at the trial the following day.

Q: So you were asked to back date a notary as if you were present, and then testify at trial that you were present when they were signed?

A: That is correct.

When Kenneth Labowitz took the stand, six days later, he flatly contradicted Cain's statement that he didn't know why he had been subpoenaed and that he had never seen the superseding contracts before. Labowitz testified that he had spoken on the telephone with Cain, who had been "very helpful, very forthcoming, and very patient in explaining to me how all these things happened. . . . Mr. Cain was generally conversant in what it is that had gone on with Mr. Bailes and these people in New York, Mr. Manfredi, Mr. Boccagna, and Mr. Zinke, and

specifically related to these two contracts. Mr. Cain told me
that he was present in Mr. Smith's law office in Abingdon when
these two contracts were typed up . . . [and] remembered
putting them in an envelope, either Federal Express or
overnight express mail, and sending them to Mr. Manfredi in
New York, and then getting them back a couple days later
either by Federal Express or express mail with a signature
affixed to them."

However, Labowitz confirmed Cain's account of being
alone with Sheila in his hotel room. It was his wedding anniver-
sary on the night in question, he said, and he could come to the
hotel to talk to his witness only after his celebratory dinner—
and after Sheila's arrival. Hulkower, in his closing statement,
made much of this piece of defense testimony, which had
served his side so well: "Think about what [Labowitz] said and
how that corroborates Mack Cain's story. Mr. Labowitz said
that he needed to meet with Mack Cain later in the evening.
Sheila McGough didn't need to meet with him at all but when
Ken Labowitz gets to the hotel room . . . Sheila McGough is
already there and they have already had a conversation. There
was no need for it. The story fit, ladies and gentlemen. . . . "

Hulkower then delivered his coup: "Now lest there be any
doubt that Sheila McGough asked Mack Cain to perjure himself, remember the testimony of Linda Cooley: After not speaking to Sheila McGough for two years, Linda Cooley gets a
sweet, friendly letter from a woman who never gave her a smile,
never gave her the time of day, who asked for a little favor.
Could she please just notarize this old photocopy of a signature
and, oh, by the way, just leave the date off so the other date
looks valid. It's just the same thing Sheila McGough asked
Mack Cain to do. And just like Mack Cain told you, he got suspicious when Sheila McGough started being chatty about his
wife and his kids, well, Linda Cooley got suspicious when
Sheila McGough started talking about sticky buns, and the

good times they had, when they never had any good times together at all."

*The story fit, ladies and gentlemen.* Trials are won by attorneys whose stories fit, and lost by those whose stories are like the shapeless housecoat that truth, in her disdain for appearances, has chosen as her uniform. It was true that Labowitz came late to the hotel room and found Sheila and Cain there together. It was true that Sheila had written a friendly letter to Linda Cooley, in which she asked her to notarize a document and mentioned a local Krispy Kreme bakery. It was not true that Sheila had asked Cain to falsely notarize the superseding contracts on the eve of trial; since copies of the contracts were already part of the court record of the case, it was out of the question that she would have done so. It was also not true that she had asked Cooley to do anything dishonest; she had asked her to renotarize a signature on a copy of a document giving her power of attorney from Bailes, of which the original was lost. But Hulkower's elegant story prevailed over the disorderly stories Kohlman and Rochon were reduced to telling in their cross-examinations: stories about Mack Cain's bad history as an employee of the Virginia Department of Rehabilitation; his involvement with Bailes in the selling of the charters; his discharge from the employ of Strother Smith; and the oddness of Sheila's assuming he would have his notary seal with him when he came to Alexandria to testify at a trial without knowing why he had been summoned.

SHEILA FINISHED the dishes and arrived in the living room just as I was asking Irene if she had meant it literally when she said that our Justice Department is like the KGB. "I disagree with my mother," Sheila said. "I think we have to make a distinction. The difference between the government of the United States of America, including the Justice Department, and that of China, to take a contemporary example, is so great that it's a difference of kind, not just of degree."

"Janet asked me a question, and I'm going to answer it," Irene said.

"I'm sorry," Sheila said.

"I will stick by my statement," Irene said. "I think in this country we have a KGB type of Justice Department. Yes. I'll stick with it. They can send me up the river if they want."

Sheila laughed and said, "Oh, I don't think they'll want you, Mother."

"Sheila, you've said enough. Be quiet. I have to think of the other thing I want to tell her."

Sheila looked fondly at her mother as Irene launched into a story about her fierce intervention when Sheila was attacked by another inmate in prison. "She was really injured and in the infirmary, and I called Senator Byrd's office and raised bloody hmnn hmnn hmnn. That was the second time she was attacked, and something had to be done." Sheila had already told me something about her experience of prison, and I recalled her mention of a fight she had had with an inmate over the noise of a radio. She had kept her tone light when speaking about prison, presenting it as a not pleasant but not terrible experience. She had spoken of her time in a jail in Oklahoma which was run as a private, profit-making enterprise and thus starved the prisoners, with the wry humorousness of someone reporting on a dismal restaurant. (The Oklahoma jail was an inexplicable way station between the Fairfax, Virginia, jail, where she was received in custody, and a minimum-security federal prison in Alderson, West Virginia, where she finished her term.) Irene was less amused. "I was angry," she went on, "and I said to Byrd, 'That piece of pork down there is beginning to smell.' And do you know, that night they took her out of the infirmary and transferred her to Kentucky." Irene told of another incident, when she came to the prison and found Sheila ill, and "they threatened to book me and put me in prison because I raised hmnn hmnn hmnn about it. She was in solitary, as sick as could be, with a light hanging down over her head, with no medical attention. Why? She wasn't a murderess. Why?"

I said that I felt for her. "If my daughter went to prison, I don't know what I would do."

"I'll tell you what you do. I hope it never happens. But be sure you call her every day, no matter how much it costs. We sent money, we visited, we called every day."

The next morning, Sheila picked me up at my hotel, and we drove to Saint Rita's Catholic Church for the Easter service; Irene and Tom had gone in their own car. The service was festive and brisk. The church was full of lilies and nicely dressed people, among them many young couples with children. A plump, rosy priest delivered a practiced and enjoyable homily, which began with the question "What did you worry about this week?" The priest confided that he himself had worried about the move of the church's Silver Spring office: "Would we get the packing done in time?" The homily ended on a reassuring note: Thanks to the remarkable event being celebrated that day, "you have nothing to worry about." During the reading of the passage in the gospel of John reporting Mary's discovery of the disappearance of Christ's body from the tomb, a fanciful analogy between Bailes and Christ floated into my mind. Hadn't Jesus, too, been selling a kind of unregulated insurance? I remembered something said to me by a man named Fred Quarles, a money broker from Charlottesville, Virginia, who had been another respondent to the *Wall Street Journal* ad of June 13: "For the normal person, who never chases after treasure ships, a guy like Bailes comes across as a con man. For someone like me, who is an adventurer at heart and has the curiosity that would kill three or four cats, it was just an interesting deal." I glanced over at Sheila, dressed in a pretty, long flowered dress, who had the same rapt and happy look on her face as the one she had bestowed on her mother on Ash Wednesday. The interesting deal of Christianity, with its minuscule down payment and its grotesquely outsize dividend, is a constantly felt presence in her life. The roots of her illusion that Bailes was an unfortunate who had fallen by the wayside and needed help from a good Samaritan like herself are surely entwined with her habit of faith. I remember once asking her if she had ever been tempted to abandon Bailes, and she had said, "Oh, yes. Giving up and abandoning Bobby was always a temptation. But I would rise above it and do what seemed to me the more ethical and honorable, the more honorable and difficult, thing." By the time of her indictment, the rest of her law practice had fallen away and she was working only for Bailes, fulfilling the obligation she felt she had incurred when she lost his false Social Security number and bank fraud case. To see the hopelessness of that case was simply beyond her ken; and somehow beside the point.

After church, Sheila and I (her parents following in their car) drove to a shopping mall, to a restaurant locally famous for its breakfasts. Not everyone's pulse quickens at the thought of a plate of scrambled eggs edged with strips of bacon and triangles of toast; there are those who can read the word "waffles" without a stab of delight. But those for whom the first meal of the day is imaginatively fused with the idea of promise and hope and things before they are spoiled will understand the réclame of the Western Sizzlin' restaurant on Lee Highway outside Alexandria. Here the art of the American breakfast is practiced with beautiful attentiveness and utter authority, and here no known American breakfast dish appears to have been overlooked. The first-time visitor can scarcely believe his eyes as he enters and sees the enormous horseshoe-shaped buffet on which every imaginable thing to eat in the morning is arrayed. Because of her impaired eye, Irene remained at the table (black waiters brought and constantly refilled cups of coffee) and allowed Sheila to fetch her breakfast from the buffet. Tom, I noticed, had passed up the eggs and potatoes and meats and fish, and had piled his plate with pastries smeared with glutinous fruit. "Doc has a sweet tooth," Irene had said at dinner, by way of explaining her husband's unusual habit of sprinkling his strawberries with jelly beans instead of sugar. Again, Tom said scarcely a word, as Irene prattled on and Sheila and I played our obedient-daughter roles. When Sheila drove me to the train station, I asked if her father was always so silent, and she said, "He says he learns more by listening than by talking. He's a very impressive talker when he talks. When he's with his medical colleagues, he can hold forth." Her own and her mother's ceaseless speech, she implied, was as nothing, was "just talk," devalued currency, in the light of the father's golden male silence. In a house of weak, chattering women, he was the powerful, silent man. Now, to be sure, he was as powerless as his wife against the insults of age. Soon after Easter he was taken to the hospital, when a heart ailment, which had been treated by surgery, renewed its depredations.

KENNETH LABOWITZ, a vital, fast-talking man in his late forties, who had represented Sheila in the MacDonald lawsuit (he replaced Joseph Roberts, the lawyer originally provided by the insurance company), received me in a nondescript conference room of the small Alexandria law firm in which he is a partner, and said of the Manfredi-Boccagna-Bailes-Zinke-MacDonald transaction: "The people involved in this deal were straight out of Damon Runyon. I mean, who were these guys? Kirkpatrick MacDonald and Frank Manfredi and Francis Boccagna and Philip Zinke. Who were they? How did they get together? This was the question we kept asking ourselves. MacDonald's story was just unbelievable. MacDonald, who went to the Sorbonne and the University of Geneva and Yale, in with all these guys: Manfredi, an unfrocked lawyer who had been prosecuted; Boccagna, twenty years old, doing business out of a phone booth on Long Island; Zinke, a fugitive with a five-million-dollar judgment against him. None of these people fit together. The whole deal didn't sound right. These guys were buying insurance charters that gave them the right to sell insurance without reserves. That's like printing money. What are they talking about?

"It was difficult to accept MacDonald's bona fides. There aren't a lot of investment bankers I know who hang out with the likes of the guys involved in this deal. And if you're going to send $75,000, you might want to have a little bit of paperwork. But there was no paperwork. It was not a deal that smelled good from any angle.

"The difficulty for us was that $75,000 clearly got sent to Sheila and promptly got disbursed. And we didn't have a piece of paper that we could point to which said that the money was nonrefundable and that she was supposed to disburse it upon receipt. Sheila, of course, insisted that it was a no-free-look deal and that she was not an escrow agent. I have no clue to what the truth was. The truth was not my responsibility. Representing Sheila's interest was my responsibility."

"So you think it is possible that Sheila was conspiring with Bailes to defraud people?" I said, taken aback by the coldness of Labowitz's remark. Sheila had given him permission to break his bond of confidentiality when speaking to me, but somehow I had expected the posture of loyalty to hold a bit better than this.

"No," Labowitz said. "Sheila certainly was trustworthy. But her perception was a little bad at times. She was making decisions that were just not healthy. She was a midget among giants in that crowd. These guys were professionals. They were a bunch of sharks. I wouldn't trust a single one of them. You count your fingers after you shake their hands."

I pressed my point. "Do you feel completely convinced of Sheila's integrity?"

"Of her integrity?" Labowitz stared at me in wonder.

"Yes. That she wouldn't do anything dishonest?"

"'Completely convinced of her integrity.' Whew." Labowitz laughed and went on, "At critical times in this deal, Sheila's judgment appeared to be flawed. It is inexplicable to me what she was hoping to accomplish when she took some of the actions she took on behalf of Mr. Bailes. Did she profit by it? It's real hard to see how. If her life was to be ruined in the way it has been ruined, it would be nice if she had at least made some money out of the deal. Or if she had had some deep romantic attachment to Mr. Bailes—which she has absolutely denied to me.

"She was coming apart at the time of the civil case. I mean, emotionally. It was unpleasant to watch. The civil case, from what I could tell, was more upsetting to her than the criminal case. In the criminal case, she had a goal and a sort of focus that she didn't have in the civil case. The civil case was one of the most unpleasant experiences I ever had as a practicing lawyer. MacDonald's lawyer was an extremely unpleasant guy. Wow. Talk about someone who was over the top, Mike Wyatt certainly was. As it turned out, the civil trial never got started. We picked a jury, and then the judge called us all to the bench and said to me, 'We're going to settle this case now.' And I said, 'Okay, great.' Jury trials are risky. Juries don't like lawyers. We didn't have a whole lot to throw up to overcome the general attitude that lawyers are sharp characters, and would you really send $75,000 on a no-free-look basis to someone you'd never met for a bunch of these insurance charters that may or may not have any value? That's a pretty difficult story for a bunch of very well-educated jurors—as we have in that court—to buy, and a tough story to sell. I had two witnesses on my side: Sheila and Mack Cain. And that's pretty thin. I thought Sheila was going to be a terrible witness. She felt personally offended by what was going on, and she was beginning to come apart. I was very concerned about what she would say when she testified."

I asked Labowitz what he would have done in Sheila's place when the $75,000 arrived.

"If I'm getting money," he replied, "I would want to know what everyone in the deal thinks I'm doing with it. It would not have been inappropriate for her to disburse the money the way she did if she had been authorized to do so by the buyers, if that's what everyone's understanding had been. But boy, I would want to make sure I had some unequivocal paperwork. I would want something in writing from everybody involved—so you can avoid situations like this. Obviously, now we would send faxes to each other. That was in the pre-fax era.

"These guys were professionals. Everybody was a shark. And Sheila was a poor little fish who was just swimming in a very tough piece of water. I don't think they were looking to catch Sheila. I think they were looking to catch each other. And Sheila happened to be the one in the middle. When the music stopped, she was the one who didn't have a chair to sit down in.

"She's got $75,000 in her hand and not a clue how to protect herself from having this blow up on her. Because she didn't know enough to send letters. She should have sent letters saying, 'I've received the money and I'm disbursing it per your instructions.' And she didn't do it. Even when the flames began to lap up against her, she doesn't have the good sense to start writing demanding letters that made reference to specific phone calls.

"Sheila didn't have any filters. She came from a proper, solid upper-middle-class good Catholic family. She had never dealt with the kinds of people she was representing, and certainly never with anyone like Bob Bailes. Bailes was a sociopath. Nothing against Mr. Bailes. That's what he did. But Sheila didn't have the ability to say, 'Wait a minute, I'm doing a little bit too much for this character. Maybe I need to look out for Sheila McGough.' It's sad. There's a tragedy here. Obviously, it's still being played out today if she can't see that she did something wrong, that she took no action to protect herself.

"In the mid-eighties, there was a group of lawyers here who were representing indigent criminal defendants—there is no public defender in Alexandria—and making names for themselves as very aggressive, take-no-prisoners, bring-everything-to-trial types. These were Sheila's role models. She followed their ethic of going right to the limit for the client. Not just in Bailes's case. Even before she got to Bailes, she would take a little case, not politically or economically rewarding—just some guy who had broken into a house and was getting prosecuted for it—and she would be all over it, going full bore at it.

"She was always by herself, never in a law firm. She never had anyone who would say to her, 'Are you sure this is where you want to be?' Sheila became known for a zealousness that was a little tough to fathom. She would see virtues in cases no one else could see. She would take on a cause and flog it to death. She was like a lawyer on TV. Lawyers on TV only have one client. That's not reality. You have to have other clients. At some point, you've got to say, 'I'm done with this, I'm not going to do that. I'm done with Bob Bailes. I've done everything for Bob Bailes that Bob Bailes deserves to have done, or that he can afford.' Because we're in business. I'm taking two hours away from charging people money to represent them—which is what I do—to talk to you. At some point—since I can't spend the rest of my life talking to you—I've got to do something else. Sheila was never able to make that kind of apportionment. She believes that if you represented your client, you represented your client.

"Even putting the best face on it, Sheila made choices she shouldn't have made. She was self-destructive at times, without a doubt. It's the stuff of tragedy that she got herself in and couldn't get herself out. And nobody said to her, 'Sheila, stop doing this. This is wrong.'

"One of the problems with our system of legal education is that you need to be diligent and responsible to get into law school, but you don't have to have a lot of worldly experience. I was practicing law when I was twenty-four, and I didn't know anything about the real world. I had contact with people like Bailes, and I got scammed, though not to the extent that Sheila was. I had never dealt with anybody who had committed a felony. Once, sitting at a table like this, I had a client explain to me how he had killed a woman with his bare hands. I was sitting there and thinking: I have no context for this. I know no way of responding to this person who is describing killing another human being. I didn't know how to respond to it. What are you supposed to say? 'That's interesting. And then what did you do?'

"In law school, they don't teach you how to maintain a distance, how to look out for yourself. And lawyers are not taught how to bill. That's a whole field in itself. You develop the attitude that it's somehow wrong to make people pay for services. Lawyers are typically uncomfortable talking about money with clients. On TV, lawyers never ever talk about money. Perry Mason used to ask for a dime: 'Here, give me a dime. Now I'm your lawyer.' Lawyers on TV never ever say, 'I'm going to represent you. You need to pay me lots of money.' We're not trained to say to someone, 'I'm all dressed up, I love going to court, I'm ready to go, I can do a good job for you, but you've got to pay me, and if you won't pay me, I won't go.' Sheila could have said, 'I'm sorry you're having all these problems, Bob Bailes, but I can't afford to help you. You're going to suck too much of my time and effort. I'm not going to do that if you don't pay me.' And Sheila never learned that. Sheila just didn't get it. Guys like Bob Bailes can suck every possible minute out of a lawyer like Sheila McGough. They know how. It's like oxygen to Bob Bailes.

"She was failed by her training, and the profession failed her by not trying to help her out. Nobody did. I didn't, and I was among the people who were closest to her. She didn't want it—that's another problem. She allowed herself to be destroyed by Bailes because she didn't learn that there's a perspective and a distance to keep and that there's a reason you're the guy's lawyer and not the guy's brother."

I said, "Have you ever had a discussion like this with Sheila?"

"No."


On a preternaturally hot day in May 1996, I took a train to Garden City, Long Island, and then a taxi to an address—300 Garden City Plaza—I read to the driver from a crumpled piece of paper in my purse: a copy of Alan Morris's telephone bill dated July 19, 1986, and marked "Plaintiff's Exhibit 13A." I had called the number on the bill a few months earlier and learned it was out of service and, further, that no Alan D. Morris was listed in Garden City or anywhere else on Long Island. Now, impelled by the notion that places can speak of what happened in them, I had come to take a look at the office where so much of the business that led to Sheila's conviction had been conducted.

In my imagination, I saw 300 Garden City Plaza as one of those handsomely plain brick office buildings erected in the 1910s or '20s that Edward Hopper liked to paint in morning light; and Room 252, Morris's office, as a modest work space furnished with a wood desk with a green blotter, a metal file cabinet, a sheaf of dusty lawbooks, accretions of objects of vague utility (a piece of screening, bottles of Parker's ink), a degree from a small law school, and black-and-white photographs, taken at ceremonial dinners, of pudgy, watchful men. My plan was to go to Room 252 and pretend to be looking for Alan Morris. While the present occupant or his secretary patiently explained that Morris had moved out years before, I would look sharply about me. I would get an idea of the place where Morris, Manfredi, and Boccagna had gathered when they plotted their course with Bailes and Bernice Kelly and Zinke and MacDonald, and then with poor Sheila. I would flesh out my sense of the milieu of these "people on Long Island" whom MacDonald had threatened and subdued.

My taxi sped along a highway for a mile or so, then turned into a huge and almost deserted shopping mall and pulled up in front of a white, five-story modern office building of utter, almost insulting bland ugliness, with the number 300 on it. A large sign near the entrance announced "Offices for Rent." I watched the taxi drive away and felt the silence and emptiness of the place. The vast spaces of the mall's parking lot were mostly unfilled, and there were few people entering and leaving the shops that lined the other side. I hurried out of the glaring sunlight into the air-conditioned coolness of the unattended lobby of 300, where Muzak played with a kind of satiric extra-chipperness, as if somehow sensing it had found its true audience: no one. A large white object—a "divider"—held artificial plants that contrived to look like untended real plants.

I took the elevator to the second floor, where there were many empty offices and suites whose doors stood open to the corridor. I couldn't find Room 252 and eventually realized that it had been absorbed by one of the vacated suites. I walked into a unit of six low-ceilinged rooms, empty of everything except institutional carpeting and venetian blinds. I moved from room to room and from window to window, whose view never changed, was always of the parking lot. I peered into corners and even scrutinized the soundproofed ceiling, looking for the small unconsidered thing from which journalistic insight is derived. But there was no such thing here. There was no trace of anyone; not even a workman's soda can had been left behind. Then I found it: the vacant rooms were themselves the treasure I sought. They gave me my metaphor for the narratives of the law—the stories told by lawyers—with which I had been trying to come to terms and which had filled me with the kind of boredom and alienation I now felt. Law stories are empty stories. They take the reader to a world entirely constructed of tendentious argument, and utterly devoid of the truth of the real world, where things are allowed to fall as they may. Trial law shares a vocabulary with science—"fact," "evidence," "proof"—but its method is the opposite of scientific method; the experiment is always fixed. The method of adversarial law is to pit two trained palterers against each other. The jury is asked to guess not which side is telling the truth—it knows that neither is—but which side is being untruthful in aid of the truth. No one has thought of a better system, but everyone who has participated in it—whether as defendant, defense lawyer, plaintiff, plaintiff's lawyer, prosecutor, judge, or juror—has gained a sense of its cynicism and absurdism.

A few weeks after the trip to Garden City, I found my trace of Morris, the "lawyer of unimpeachable credentials," as Hulkower called him in one of his reply briefs to Abrams. An acquaintance at the Departmental Disciplinary Committee of the New York State Supreme Court, whom I had called on a hunch, sent me the court order disbarring Morris for stealing escrow funds from a client. A month later, I learned that in 1993 Morris was sentenced to a year in prison for, among other things, stealing thousands of dollars' worth of savings bonds from an old woman and forging the signature on a promissory note for $130,000.

# PART II

I N APRIL 1996, I traveled to Abingdon, Virginia, to speak with S. Strother Smith, one of the many lawyers whom Bob Bailes employed (as sort of studio assistants) over the years and who had appeared as a witness for the defense at Sheila's criminal trial. The man who met my noon plane at a small airport on the border of Tennessee, Kentucky, and Virginia was in his mid-fifties, bearded and slight of build, and immensely affable and obliging. He had a characteristic American humorous manner—the manner shared alike by the humorous and deeply humorless among us—and was wearing an uncharacteristic (for that time of day in that part of the country) dark-blue pin-striped suit. Smith no longer practices law; he was ordained as an Anglican priest in 1987 and now divides his time between his pastoral duties and Republican Party politics. At the time of my visit, he was running for the party office of district chairman and wore a yellow button in his lapel advertising his candidacy. As we drove to Abingdon, sixty miles away, Smith gave me the history of his service with Bailes.

"I first met Bob when I came to Abingdon in 1970 to practice law. I was young and obviously inexperienced—which was the type of lawyer Bob preferred to deal with—and like any young lawyer, I was hungry for clients. Bob came in with a lot of talk about all the money he had. He was doing something with some coal mines in West Virginia, and he wanted me to sign off on some land titles, but without doing the title search. He was a thoroughly unscrupulous type of a guy. But I didn't know that at the time. Then he came to me to represent him in Treasure Mountain. This was a housing development he had going up. He said he had the financing for it but needed to borrow some additional money. He wanted me to call the Virginia National Bank in Abingdon about a loan and, as his lawyer, to verify that he had the long-term financing for his project. For my own verification, he said I could call this bank in Atlanta and ask for a certain executive vice president, who would confirm that Bob had the long-term financing. I called the number he gave me and asked for the vice president, and he said that, yes, they knew Bob, and that Bob had a credit line of ten million dollars, or whatever it was supposed to be, and, yes, they wanted him to have local construction money. Now, my wife has a more suspicious nature than I do—I tend to be rather accepting of people—and she said, 'Well, you know how Bob has been in these other things. Why don't you call Information and make sure that number is the number of the bank.' I've always kidded her about how she must have a criminal mind to think like that, but I did what she said and, lo and behold, the number of the bank in Atlanta was not the number he had given me. He had given me another number. I had no idea who I had called. When I called the bank's real number, they had never heard of Bailes."

"Did you confront him?" I asked.

"Yes, and he said that the bank had several different offices and I must have got the wrong one."

"He was very fast on his feet, wasn't he?"

"Oh, yes. He always had an explanation, and he was so convincing that though you knew to be on your guard, you never knew for sure that what he was saying wasn't right. I still don't know whether the insurance companies were legitimate. Bob also had all sorts of physical problems, and anytime he needed an excuse for something, he could always generate a symptom that required him to be in the hospital or in a doctor's office—so that he never was in court or anywhere else when he didn't want to be. I think the feds finally figured that out."

"Did he talk his way back into your good graces after your call to the fake bank?"

"Yes. I wanted to represent Bob. He was always nice. I never saw him angry. He was a nice guy. He could always ingratiate himself. He was not real good-looking, but he was quite a charmer. And he sounded like some of his business things might offer a real opportunity, though I never knew how far you could trust him and suspected you couldn't. He somehow got the loan for Treasure Mountain and began to develop the property, but then he defaulted on the loan, and the bank took over and developed the property itself. I finally had to break with Bob. At one point, when I was out of town, traveling, he actually moved into my office with a secretary, and when I returned I discovered that he had prepared a bunch of pleadings and signed my name to them. When I confronted him, he said, 'You signed those pleadings—don't you remember?' and I said, 'No, Bob. In the first place, on that date, I was at trial in Pikesville, Kentucky, and in the second place, there's a certain way I've been signing my name in the last two years.' After I was ordained, I always signed my name with a cross after it, and none of these pleadings had a cross. Otherwise, it would have been hard for me to tell it wasn't my signature. He was an excellent forger. I said, 'Sorry, Bob, that's it. You're out of here. I don't want you back.'"

I asked Smith about his orientation as a Republican, and he said, "I've been told that I'm to the right of Attila the Hun. I'm a very, very strong believer in the Constitution as written. I have three daughters, and by the time they were twelve years old, all three of them knew how to use a gun. I'm a life member of the NRA. I'm very much opposed to any form of gun control. When my dad graduated from college, a member of my family, who lived in Belgium, sent him a very fine shotgun.

When the Nazis came in, they had that relative's name on a list of people who had bought shotguns, and they came to him and demanded that he give them the shotgun. When he couldn't produce it, they shot him. That's the way they were able to set up their dictatorship. The ultimate defense for democracy is an armed populace. The Second Amendment says the people have the right to bear arms. I would never vote for anyone who was for any sort of gun control, period. I'm very, very pro-life. I believe that anyone who says, 'I'm personally against abortion, but . . . ,' is being intellectually dishonest."

We had turned off the interstate and were driving through beautiful farm country. It was an overcast day, and a mist hovered over the fields and swirled through the old trees. As we neared Abingdon, a pre-Revolutionary town, it began to rain. Smith's office was opposite a gas station on a stretch of highway outside the historic district. It was in a two-story white frame house he had bought in 1980 and converted into offices. Since discontinuing his law practice, he has rented out some of the offices and donated others to the local Republican Party organization. The place had a disordered, disheveled, transitional air. Smith's conversion of the house into an office building had largely consisted of covering all the interior walls with the laminated-wood paneling that is a kind of uniform for rural offices; now, with only a few remnants of office furniture remaining, the rooms looked out of kilter. The first room we entered, formerly a reception area, was empty, except for piles of clothing and boxes of miscellaneous stuff—the belongings of a daughter who was in the military, Smith said, and about to leave for the Middle East. In another room, Republican campaign literature lay about in haphazard stacks. I picked up a flyer printed on bright-yellow paper, which began:

Dear Fellow Republican(s):
    In the fall of 1996 we are going to be faced with one of the most, if not the most, crucial elections in our nation's

history. We will be deciding if we will enter the 21st century with more and more power over our lives and hard-earned tax money belonging to a "Big Brother" national government under "liberal" Democrats, or if we will be living in a society that prizes individual liberty, free enterprise, and a maximally efficient and minimally taxing and interfering government, as was envisioned by our forefathers when our great nation began.

Smith pointed out his own former office and also showed me a large room that Mack Cain had occupied. I asked Smith to tell me about Cain, and he said, "Mack Cain, as I eventually found out, had something of the same personality as Bob, though on a much lower level. I had never had to fire anybody in my life, but I had to let him go, because I found out that he was actually on Bob's payroll and doing what Bob wanted him to do. Before Mack came to me he had worked as a vocational specialist for the Virginia Department of Vocational Rehabilitation, and they fired him for lying and for filing false documents."

"How did he come to be working for you?"

"He was a neighbor. He had lost his job, and his family was going to lose their home, and I needed a legal assistant, so I hired him. After I dismissed him, I didn't oppose his applying for unemployment compensation. I tried to help him, to the extent I could. I could have gone in to the authorities and said, 'I didn't lay him off, I fired him, because he did things I told him not to do.' I could have prevented him from getting the unemployment insurance and saved myself about five thousand dollars in increased unemployment taxes for the next year."

"But you were merciful to him."

"Yes."

Smith had testified late in Sheila's trial and had not heard Mack Cain's testimony. When I told him what Cain had said, and what Sheila and Labowitz said in contradiction, he replied,

"I suspect it was Mack doing the lying. When he worked for me, and I confronted him with the things he had done, he didn't hesitate to lie about them. Mack's wife, Betty, once said to my wife—by then, Mack and Betty had split up and he had left the area—that there was one thing about Mack she could never deal with and that was his inability to tell the truth. My wife, who is getting a doctorate in psychology, used the term 'pathological liar' about him. And that, ultimately, was the reputation he gained in this area."

We returned to the car, and Smith proposed a drive around the county to the various places where Bailes had lived and operated. Abingdon, with its restored pre-Revolutionary brick houses and expensive hotel and famous Barter Theatre and elegant shops and galleries, was a discrepancy, a kind of false note, in the landscape of housing developments put up on the cheap, and blunt commercial strips, by which it was hedged—our authentic, amiably ugly American landscape. Some remnants of farm country remained between the developed places, and as we drove along a pretty country road leading to the town of Glade Spring, Smith deplored the rain that prevented the mountains from coming into view. In Glade Spring, Smith pointed out an old frame house that Bailes, before he went to prison, had told him he was going to buy and use as an office; and then a split-level brick house that Bailes had built in the seventies and had lived in with his first wife, Barbara, and their daughter, Leigh. "Barbara is still here," Smith said. "She teaches in the Washington County school system. She is a very nice, responsible person. His second wife, Lynette, was much younger, very sophisticated. I never met her. What I know about her is what Bob told me—that she was always interested in how she looked, going to the best beauty salons and taking Bermuda cruises. She divorced him in 1985."

We left Glade Spring and headed for Treasure Mountain, the failed development, in the nearby town of Emory, where

Bailes had gone to Emory and Henry College, a small Methodist institution. On the way, Smith slowed down to point to a development of small, identical ranch-style houses set on uniform lots. "This here is Country Club Estates," he said. "It's pretty well typical of the housing that came along when Bob was working in real estate here in the seventies. These are just your middle-class homes, running fifty, sixty thousand dollars. And this is not what Bob had in mind for Treasure Mountain. He had a whole lot of more grandiose ideas."

Smith then proposed that we make a brief detour and see another development, whose level of pretension was more commensurate with Bailes's ideas. We presently arrived at the exemplary grandiose development, which was called Winterham, and whose site, on a hillside formerly pastureland, commanded a panoramic view of the now absent mountains. I don't think I have ever been to an odder place. The twenty houses that had just gone up here were a far cry from the humble ranch houses of Country Club Estates. They were huge, looming mansions, with seven or eight bedrooms each. Designed in various period styles—Colonial, Greek Revival, Victorian, Tudor, Beaux Arts—no two were alike. There were houses with Corinthian columns, houses with turrets, houses with mansard roofs and elaborate cornices and pilasters, houses made of brick or stucco or wood; houses that stuck to a single style and houses that were pastiches of several styles. But what gave the place its surreal appearance was not the houses themselves but their extreme closeness to one another, as if they were huddling together. Houses that should have been surrounded by gardens and orchards and allées of lindens and deer parks were only yards apart, built on lots the size of the lots at Country Club Estates. The effect of this cramming was to give the Winterham ensemble the look of a sample book of architectural style—or of an ironic postmodernist gesture. Smith pointed out the golf course and the swimming pool and the clubhouse that were part of the deal of living in fantastical Winterham. He said that most of the houses had been sold—to executives in the neighboring coal towns. Bailes's plans for Treasure Mountain had evidently been made with these executives in mind and had been similarly grand. In actuality—as with everything Bailes touched—the scheme had dissolved into nothing.

"This is Treasure Mountain up here," Smith said. We had pulled off the main road and onto a tributary dirt road leading to a wooded hillside. "I haven't been up here since it was taken over by the bank and developed, so I have no idea what they did and how much, if anything, of Bob's dream for it was realized." We began to climb the hill. It was a bleak and desolate spot. Scraggly second-growth trees and brush, not yet in leaf, grew along the roadside, here and there punctuated by a small, cheap brick house. "It doesn't look like they've done much," Smith said.

"Those are rather modest houses," I said, the mansions of Winterham still in my head.

"These are not the type of houses Bob envisioned. They aren't anything like the houses he had in his drawings. But when the bank foreclosed on the property, all they wanted was to get their money out of it, so they built what was most salable. These are probably thirty-, forty-thousand-dollar homes." He added, "Bob was going to have a golf course and a swimming pool and a clubhouse. I think he had actually started building the pool, but I don't know where it is." Before we reached the top of the hill, Strother Smith said, "Well, you get the idea," and turned back down, past the charmless houses and their equally unprepossessing natural surroundings. On the highway again, he began to speak of Sheila. "But for the grace of God— and possibly my wife's intuition—I might have been in the same boat," he said. "When I saw Sheila at her criminal trial I was shocked by her appearance. She was a very attractive young lady when I first saw her. At the criminal trial she looked twenty years older than I am."

I asked Smith how he had first come to meet Sheila. His answer gave me something of the feeling of unreality that Winterham had produced. "I'm very strongly opposed to the use of Social Security numbers as identification," he replied, and went on, "I've never given my Social Security number to anyone but the IRS. It's against my religious beliefs. In the Bible, every time God blessed someone, He named him, and every time He cursed somebody, He numbered him. The worst sin David ever committed was not the sin of adultery with Bathsheba, or the sin of killing her husband, Uriah, but the sin of numbering the people of Israel. Throughout the Bible, it tells of this being a major violation of one's relationship to God. So if I'm asked for a Social Security number, I won't give it—if necessary, I'll make up a number. Well, Bob had a case where he was charged with using the wrong Social Security number for defrauding a bank or something of the sort, and knowing of my religious beliefs and of my work on getting legislation passed that would allow people to refuse to let their Social Security number be used as the number of their Virginia driver's license, he asked me to come up to Alexandria and testify for him. Sheila was representing him, and that's how I first met her."

An appendix to the record of that trial contains an affidavit by Smith that starts out: "In Revelation and, indeed, throughout the Old Testament, the name of God is glorified and the names of those who follow him are glorified, whereas identification of people by number is always the mark of the Devil, Baal, and Maloch. . . . In all of the history of mankind, the name of a person was expected to describe the person or bring a blessing upon the person. No number can do that. Therefore, any Christians who understand the concept of the name-blessing and the taking away of the name and replacing it with a curse do not, and cannot, in the light of their very sincerely held religious views, give the same number for every commercial transaction, and many have severe problems even using the Social Security number for governmental and tax purposes."

In his oral trial testimony, however, Smith did not go into any of this. His task was to support the legitimacy of a most illegitimate-looking document: a copy of a letter Bailes said he had received from the Department of Health and Human Services. The letter (which was unsigned and titled "Memo") read:

Dear Mr. Bailes,

We are now continuing to investigate the misuse of your Social Security number, and until this matter is cleared up, you are to use the above number and not the old one.

We have corrected the spelling of your last name, and I have now placed an "i" in it, and have also corrected your date of birth to 5/6/40 instead of 6/5/40.

This investigation has now been going on since 1976, and now after six years, I feel that something should be completed in a short time.

The use of this new number will in no way cause you to have to start all over paying in benefits, as you will be given credit for all previous payments.

You can take this letter to the proper places and they will correct your number, so that this will not in any way cause you difficulty.

The investigation will have to be completed before all the changes will go into the data system, so do not be up set if it does take a while. This matter will be transferred to Virginia within a few weeks, and someone from the office there will contact you.

This remarkable letter was clearly another of Bailes's cut-and-paste jobs. (The letter in evidence was, of course, a Xerox copy.) A real letter from the Department of Health and Human Services provided the letterhead, and a time-and-date stamp (available at any stationer) gave the document its look of bureaucratic verisimilitude. But, as with all of Bailes's works, the execution was not up to the conception. Underneath the letterhead was the telltale edge line that copiers inscribe when they copy pasted material; and the happy inspiration of the stamped date proved to be not so happy after all, since, as the prosecutor wearily pointed out, dates are stamped on letters received, not sent. Even Sheila has reluctantly conceded to me that she does not believe the letter to be real; I had to press hard to get this concession from her, but she couldn't say otherwise. The letter was as fake as the dirty dishes and dirty clothes in the car were real. But what a delightful fantasy wafts out of it! What a nice man it was who wrote it! How thoughtful and considerate he is! He doesn't brush supplicants away, as other bureaucrats do, but tries to be helpful and useful. He believes Bailes's story that a migrant worker named Pedro Gomez—an alien from Mexico—has been using his Social Security number, so he needs a new one. He has stepped in where his predecessors were careless and lax, and now, "after six years," is going to quickly do what needs to be done. The process of getting a new Social Security number will be easy and pleasant ("this will not in any way cause you difficulty"), but should there be delay, "do not be up set." This endlessly obliging bureaucrat reminds one of someone—of Sheila, of course—but also of other lawyers Bailes sucked into his vortex and mesmerized into preternatural forbearance. Smith's testimony at the trial (he said he had himself received unsigned and ungrammatical letters from the Social Security Administration) was ineffectual; and his remarks about the Devil, Baal, and Maloch evidently left the judge unmoved as well.

As we drove past the manicured grounds of Emory and Henry College, Smith said, "Bob was real smart and real well-read. I guess he had plenty of time to read when he was in prison."

"What kind of books did he read?"

"He read most of C. S. Lewis—the Narnia series. He could discuss the theological aspects of Tolkien's hobbits. He could discuss the Council of Nicea, which was the basis of the separation of the Eastern and Western churches. He could discuss the various forms of Arianism, one of the ancient heresies. And he could put on a cloak of religiosity, if that served his purpose. But I never considered him a religious person."

IN SEPTEMBER 1996, I traveled to the South again, to speak to two of Sheila's other predecessors in the hopeless defense of Bailes over the years. The lawyers were Birg Sergeant, of Pennington Gap, Virginia, and William Sheffield, of Abingdon. I visited Sergeant first, in the small house on Pennington Gap's Main Street that served as his law office. Sergeant, a large man with bushy, curly gray hair, an interesting European-looking face, and a friendly, courtly manner, ushered me into his conference room at the back of the house. The room had the obligatory vertical wood paneling and was in a state of comfortable disorder. It was a conference room designed on different principles from those guiding Hulkower's imposing classical-columned one, if it was designed at all. Here things were allowed to turn up, to pile up, to be pressed into service, to not match, to not impress anyone. The conference table was an old, rather beat-up, glass-top model, with an agreeable mess of papers and objects on it. There was a bookcase of lawbooks, some with very old leather covers, a serviceable blue carpet; a TV set and a video camera; and orange crates filled with papers, pushed into a corner. A dysfunctional clock sat placidly on the top of the bookcase. Among the chairs around the table were four modern chrome ones with gray upholstery, which did not match the table or the other chairs, of old-fashioned wood and leather; they had doubtless been needed as the older chairs wore out or collapsed, and not been grudged their utilitarian place at the table.

Sergeant offered me the choice of coffee or Diet Pepsi and then proceeded to speak of Bailes with the same mixture of exasperation and helpless affection that Strother Smith had displayed. "I represented him in his first significant criminal case. It was loans—he had gotten loans from a bank on fraudulent financial statements. He claimed to have assets that the bank was unable to find. We pleaded guilty, and he got probation. It was a plea agreement. He got into trouble again soon after that. He was always dealing in these grandiose schemes. Truth and reality and fantasy were all part of the same thing to him.

"In 1975, we were building a new library here and were trying to find old railroad ties. Bob told us he had railroad ties at a project he was putting up in Bristol, sixty-five miles from here, and said we could help ourselves to them—they were lying loose at the project. So several of us citizens took National Guard vehicles and equipment down to Bristol and picked up a load of Bob's railroad ties. Well, it turned out they weren't his. The bank had already foreclosed on the project, and when they saw the ties were gone, they went to some trouble to find them. They traced them to us here, and eventually they donated them to our library. This was just one of Bob's typical deals."

Sergeant, too, had been a witness for the defense at Sheila's criminal trial and had testified that he had gone to school with Bailes in the nearby town of Jonesville and had played with him when he was six. But now, when I asked him questions about Bailes's boyhood, he could tell me almost nothing; it was not Bailes but Bailes's older brother, "Mousie," who had been Sergeant's classmate and friend. Bailes had been only the uninteresting little brother. At the trial, Sergeant's wish to be helpful had caused him to slightly distort the truth. Nothing hinged on the matter—as nothing had hinged on the matter of the telephone number in the *Wall Street Journal* ad. It just made a better answer to Kohlman's "Did you ever run across a gentleman by the name of Bob Bailes?" to say, as he did, "I went to school with him, yes, sir, known him all my life, played with him when I was six years old," than to bring in "Mousie" and tell the cumbersome whole truth.

To compensate for his own paucity of memories, Sergeant had invited two women who knew Bailes in his boyhood and youth to join us at the conference table. One, in her early fifties, was Margery Halsey Coffee, whose family had lived close to the Bailes family in Jonesville; the other, a few years older, was Ora Rowlett, who had been a young teacher at the Jonesville high school when Bailes was a student there. Both women were naturally talkative—they spoke in pronounced Southern drawls—and took up their roles of informants with enthusiasm. But as the occasion wore on, it became clear that their store of memories of the young Bailes, nicknamed "Dauber" ("as in mud dauber," Sergeant explained, "which is a certain kind of wasp that lives in this area and that makes a little house, a kind of tunnel"), was as meager as Sergeant's. For Coffee, Bailes was just the "mischievous and not very nice boy" who lived across the road and with whom she had nothing to do; for Rowlett, he was a student she had not herself taught, about whom she had heard some bad things (he pilfered gum from the gum ball machine that stood outside the principal's office and jimmied the locks of lockers). As I politely leafed through a Jonesville High School yearbook Coffee had brought, she said, "Dauber was cute, maybe a little on the pudgy side, but not to any distraction," and Rowlett offered the thesis that Bailes had been bored in school and that if there had been a program for gifted children, he might have been deflected from his life of crime. "The school didn't offer enough to keep him challenged," she said.

"Did Birg tell you what happened to Dauber in college?" Coffee asked.

"No," I said, suppressing a yawn.

"I wasn't here at the time," Coffee went on, in her chatty way. "I was in school in Florida, so all this is hearsay, but it's pretty direct hearsay. One of my friends wrote me about it. When Dauber was at Emory and Henry College, there was this school pet, a little dog. Emory and Henry is close to Marion, where they have a train station, and the train tracks run through the college. The students had this pet dog—it just belonged to the students—and one day there was a group of them standing near the tracks with the dog. A train was going by, and Dauber took the dog and threw it on the train."

"What?" I said, waking up.

"And they tarred and feathered him."

"Bailes threw the dog under the train?"

"No, on the train. Onto a boxcar, so that it was carried away from campus. And they tarred and feathered him and nearly killed him. I remember getting the news that he was on the point of death."

Sergeant shook his head. "No, I think that was kind of exaggerated. He was tarred and feathered, but I think it was maple syrup rather than coal tar. They didn't have coal tar. They got the syrup from the dining hall and acquired feathers somewhere."

"He ended up in the hospital anyway," Coffee said.

"Did they ever find out what happened to the dog?" I asked.

"No," Sergeant said. "Not that I know of."

"So he wasn't real beloved by his fellow students," Coffee said.

In a final gesture of helpfulness, Sergeant telephoned the former principal of the Jonesville high school and asked if I could drop by and talk to him about his recollections of Bailes. He agreed, and after I said goodbye to Sergeant and the two women, I drove out to the principal's house in Jonesville, a small, plain two-story frame house whose white paint had turned a wan gray. The door was opened by an old woman who looked at me with suspicion, almost with hatred. When I explained my errand, she continued to stare at me wordlessly. Then she allowed me to enter the house and went to fetch the principal. A thin, very old man, who seemed ill and in pain, emerged. We sat in a living room whose walls were the color of putty and which was almost completely bare of furniture—a few ruined armchairs and wooden kitchen chairs hugged the walls at great distances from each other. The principal sank into an armchair and I pulled up a kitchen chair in order to hear him. He spoke softly and with great difficulty—he had emphysema, he told me. He wished he could be helpful, but it soon became clear that he could no longer recall anything about Dauber. I had come too late. I thanked him and took my leave. On my way out, through a door that stood ajar in the hallway and showed a darkened bedroom, I saw the suspicious old woman again, standing bent over beside the bed, taking off all her clothes.

THE NEXT day, I drove back to Abingdon and called on William Sheffield at his law office on the edge of town, where Main Street peters out to become a strip of gas stations, tractor dealers, and stores (usually closed) displaying used appliances in their dusty windows. The law office was in a one-story white house with a little lawn and a scattering of foundation plantings in front of it. Sheffield received me in his conference room, which was as utilitarian and unpretentious as Sergeant's. (There was perhaps an even greater amount of stuff that had been allowed to pile up.) Sheffield himself was quite different from the low-key and somewhat tentative Sergeant. He was a tall man, in his late seventies, who had an air of immense self-possession and confidence, and the appearance of a Mississippi gambler, with his long gray hair and white mustache, his tinted glasses, his teal-blue suit, paisley cravat, red-and-black cowboy boots, and, for raffish good measure, a few lower front teeth missing.

Sheffield related the history of his acquaintance with Bailes: "He came to me in the early seventies and asked if I could handle some legal business for him. I got more than I bargained for. At that time, he was involved in a project called Treasure Mountain. There was a mistake in the description of the land. The old gentleman who had mapped the property had been dead for years, and he had drawn the property line with a line that didn't close. Bailes wanted me to straighten this out for him, and I did. He had a grandiose scheme that looked real good on paper, and it might have worked—might have worked. I'm not going to say it would have. It might have. But he never completed it. Several buildings were built, and a sewer system was put in. He had a swimming pool built, and part of a nine-hole golf course. But the scheme came crumbling down. To be frank with you, what happened was that in some way or another, the money he borrowed—everything he did was on borrowed capital—wouldn't go far enough. There was a leak in it somewhere. It dribbled out someplace. He would always run out of money."

On the telephone, Sheffield had satirically referred to Bailes as "Honest Bob." Now I asked him how he had first become aware of Bailes's "honesty."

"What gave me my first inkling was this scheme he had over in Princeton, West Virginia. He went out there and put up in a motel and started selling coal land with tax write-offs to some of these, uh, mainly Jewish people. I'm not criticizing them—I mean, that's who he picked on. There was a law that said you could buy local coal land and if you didn't mine it you got a tax write-off some way or another. It was a very good deal. The trouble was that the land didn't have the coal it was purported to have. Bailes had misrepresented the depth of the seams. The land was worthless, in fact. I was representing Bob in these transactions, and he got me sued for a million and a half bucks. I was charged with conspiring to defraud these Jewish people by issuing erroneous title opinions. He defrauded these people—no question about it. He got a pile of money off them, using what purported to be my title opinions. Bob was a whiz with a copying machine. He'd get an example of your signature and put it on something you'd never seen. I said, 'I want to see the original.' I knew there was no original. I knew how he did it. And the judge threw the charge against me out of court."

"But you remained friendly with him, even after that," I said, recalling that Sheffield had testified for Bailes in 1986 in the bank fraud and Social Security case.

"Well, after a fashion. I didn't want to do him any harm."

"He did you harm."

"Yes, he did me some harm." Sheffield, like Smith, couldn't explain his loyalty to and liking for Bailes, in spite of everything. He added, "He was brilliant. He was a good thinker, a good organizer. But I believe what he really enjoyed was testing the system to see if he could beat it. I believe this with all my heart. The things he did, he could have wiggled out of some of them easily, and he didn't, because he wanted to see if he could beat the system. Sometimes he did and sometimes he didn't. But I think that was his goal, to see if he could do it."

"It was a game for him," I said.

"It was a game, that's right. There was another operation of his, down in Bristol, Virginia, that will give you a further idea of his shenanigans. He purportedly had a master's degree from the state university, some sixty miles from here. I know he graduated from Emory and Henry College, because that's my college, but I don't know about the master's degree. Anyway, he claimed that on the basis of the degree some agency had commissioned him to do a survey of housing, or lack thereof, in Bristol. Knowing him, I don't think anybody commissioned him to do anything. But he did this survey, which claimed that Bristol had a shortage of medium-income housing, and took it to a bank and got a loan of $900,000 to build seven medium-income apartment houses in Bristol. Well, after he had built three apartment houses and was starting on the fourth, it was discovered that the $900,000 in the account had dwindled down to $50,000. He did it by doubling every charge. If the payroll was $2,500, he drew $5,000 from the account and pocketed half. The same way with materials.

"In 1986, Bailes tried to employ me to represent him in the federal case Sheila took on. I wouldn't do it. I said, 'I'm not going to, because, number one, you haven't enough money to pay me, and, secondly, I don't have enough confidence in your case anyway. Knowing you, I would go in there with a defense they would shoot holes in right quick.' "

I told Sheffield of Sheila's feeling of guilt about her representation of Bailes in that case, of how she blamed herself for his conviction.

Sheffield, who had sat through the trial, said, "I thought she did a very respectable job. Maybe not in maneuvering. I've been doing criminal law for forty-six years, and I still don't know the ins and outs. It's really tricky, and there are so many things you can do that don't meet the eye. She wasn't up to that kind of sleight of hand. But I thought her courtroom presentation was very good for a person of her experience. I was right impressed with her, and I've seen a lot of good criminal lawyers in my time.

"When I met Sheila before the trial, at her Alexandria office in the summer of 1986, I thought she was a very nice lady. I'd give anything to have known her well enough to have warned her to be careful. After the trouble Bob caused me, I might have told her, 'Look, you go easy on this. He'll end up getting you in some kind of trouble'—which he did. That guy brought her down. I know that. I know his modus operandi. He pulled the same trick on me that he pulled on her with the $75,000 wire transfer. One day, he came to my office and said, 'Bill, I'm having some money wired to your trust account.' I said, 'For what?' and he said, 'Well, I owe you some money.' I said, 'Yeah, I know that, all right. But why the wire transfer? Why not have the person send me a check?' He said, 'No, I'm going to pay

you part of it, but I need the rest.' At that time he was purportedly doing some work for some outfit in northern Virginia, and
he said they owed him five or six thousand dollars—it wasn't a
great big amount but enough so he would pay me a thousand.
He owed me several thousand—he still owes me several thousand. But I said, 'No, I'd rather this wouldn't come to my trust
account. I'd have to account for it.' Well, without my knowing
it, he had the number of my account. He probably got it off a
check I had issued him for something. And the next day the
bank calls, and the banker says to me, 'Bill, there's a wire transfer over here for you for five thousand dollars.' I said, 'Where
from?' and he gave me the name of these people I had never
heard of—there were two names, like King and Roberts—and I
started thinking. I thought: Doggone! Bailes has done this.
That scoundrel! So I called around and finally got him on the
phone and said, 'Listen, I told you not to send the money to
me.' 'Well,' he said, 'I had to have it sent somewhere. If you
don't think it's legitimate, you call this number.' He gave me
this number of these people, and I called it and said, 'Look, how
come you wire-transferred this money to my account?' And the
person on the line said, 'Well, we did that on Mr. Bailes's
instructions.' So I said, 'Is it okay? Is there anything wrong with
it?' The person said, 'No, not a thing. It's a perfectly legitimate
deal. Just go ahead and distribute Mr. Bailes's part of it, and you
keep your part of it.' So I went ahead and did that. Well, in two
or three weeks, there's this guy who calls me up. He had some
sort of Jewish name—I can't tell, but my wife could tell they
were Jewish people. He said, 'What are you going to do about
that five thousand dollars we wired to you?' I said, 'Who are
you?' 'I'm So-and-so, with King and Roberts.' I said, 'Ah. Well,
what am I supposed to do about it?' And he says, 'We want
our money back.' This is what had happened: When Bailes
requested payment for the work he had purportedly done, he
didn't have the proper documentation to show them, so they
said they would send the money in escrow to my account and

release it when he provided the documentation. He never provided the documentation, so they wanted their money back. When I found out Sheila had been taken in the same way, it didn't surprise me. I could have told her, 'Don't accept any wire transfer from anybody in the world that Bob has had anything to do with, because you're likely to get into trouble.' "

As Sheffield said this, I felt a chill. "Why didn't you tell this story at the trial?" I said.

"I would have told them anything they asked me."

"But they didn't ask you."

"When I got up there," Sheffield said, "Mark Rochon only had a very brief conversation with me before I took the stand. Being a lawyer myself, I wasn't going to say, 'Don't you want to know about so-and-so?' I didn't do that. Maybe I should have. I thought he knew what I knew. I thought he knew enough to ask me the proper questions when I testified. But that didn't happen."

"That's a story that would have helped Sheila."

"As I say, I feel sorry for that girl. I wish I had warned her, 'For God's sake, do not let him have money wired to your account.' The last time I saw Bailes alive, I reminded him. I said, 'Bob, you ought to be completely ashamed of yourself for what you did to Sheila McGough.' He said, 'What did I do to her?' I said, 'You lying scoundrel, you know what you did to her.' And he said, 'Well, she went to jail, but it wasn't my fault.' I said, 'What do you mean, it wasn't your fault? Do you remember that trick you pulled on me about money from those fellows up in northern Virginia?' 'I don't remember.' He did. I said, 'I wish to God I had warned her.' And he went on and made up some big story about how that wasn't the way it happened, that I was all wrong, that it wasn't his fault. He tried to make it sound as if it was because of her *greed* that that had happened."

"He talked about her greed?"

"He said, like, 'Well, I guess she could use the money, and maybe she stretched a little to get it.' Stuff like that. And I said,

'You ought to be ashamed of yourself for what you did to that poor innocent girl.' He said, 'What are you talking about? What did I do? I didn't do anything.' That's the last time I saw him. I didn't want to see him anymore."

"Sheila always thought, and still thinks, of Bailes as a victim," I said.

"He was a victim of his own shenanigans, if he was a victim at all. Whatever happened, he deserved it. But that girl—that was tragic."

Kohlman and Rochon's idea in bringing Smith, Sergeant, and Sheffield to the stand had been to cite their toleration of Bailes's shenanigans as a precedent for Sheila's; but, of course, none of these lawyers had been as rash as Sheila, and the parallels Rochon and Kohlman sought to draw were easily destroyed by Hulkower's cross-examination. Sheffield had flown in on the fourth day of the trial, and he told me that he had only a vague sense of what Sheila was charged with. He said that if he had read the indictment and seen the charge relating to the $75,000 wire transfer, "naturally, I would have said, 'Let me tell you a parallel to that one.' But I didn't know about the $75,000 wire transfer then. I only know about it now because somebody sent me an article in the *Washington Post* about it."

On my way out, Sheffield introduced me to his secretary, Hilda, a woman of about forty, with platinum-blond hair, who sat at a desk at the end of a long reception room that looked like a living room, with its matching sofas, a shag rug, and a TV set. She said of Bailes, "I always enjoyed him. He was always nice to me. You couldn't help but like him. He was fun to be with, wasn't he, Bill?"

"He was always trying to get you to do something for him," Sheffield reminded her.

MY CONVERSATIONS with Sheila had fallen into a pattern. I would accuse her of blindness and naïveté about Bailes, and she would defend herself and then veer off into her theory of the government's conspiracy against her. I would say something like, "How can you talk about Bailes as a real businessman who owned real companies and dealt in millions of dollars, when he lived out of his car and kept his files in banana boxes in someone's trailer in the woods?" (The last gibe derived from a piece of testimony at Bailes's Charlotte trial by the trailer's owner, one Billy Jack Little.)

Sheila would reply, "Well, all I know is that that is in no way unlawful."

"I'm not talking about lawful," I impatiently said on one of these occasions, cutting into the speech I knew she would make. "I'm talking about what kind of feeling one has about a guy like that."

Sheila made her speech: "I didn't have feelings about my clients in that sense. I took them as they came. They had problems, and I tried to solve them. When you're in the legal business, particularly in criminal defense, you try to solve the client's legal problems. You don't say, 'Here's somebody who doesn't have an office on Main Street or Wall Street, so therefore he must be a crook and I can't or won't defend him.' It's quite possible for someone who doesn't have a conventional business—or who might have engaged in irregularities—to have his rights violated, either by other businessmen or by the government. And it's the lawyer's job to protect the interests and claims of the client. I don't see a problem with that."

"I guess the reason I keep pushing you on this point is that I want you to concede that you could have been more careful in the Manfredi-Boccagna transaction."

"Well, that's certainly possible," she said. "But we still come back to the same thing. If I had done anything illegal in that case—"

I again interrupted. "Sheila, you keep saying 'illegal.' What I'm talking about is living in the world and having some sense of who the honest people are and who the crooks are. All the people I've talked to have agreed that Bailes was a crook of some kind. Only you don't seem to see that."

Sheila serenely went on with her aria: "I don't understand how anyone could imagine that someone like Bailes, who at worst was trying to make money from other sharpies—trying to outsharp sharpies like Manfredi and MacDonald and that lot—how anyone could think that someone like that is a worse shady character than Hulkower and his boss, Henry Hudson, and his crowd, who systematically misuse the power of the United States Government and its police power to frame someone. It's an intolerable hell, in a civic sense, to live in a society where, because some people don't like you and want to see you ruined, you can be destroyed when you make a misstep, when you do something that is not unlawful but merely imprudent— even if they have to use perjury to do so. I didn't commit any crime, and they knew it from the beginning."

I had heard this so many times before. "What was their motive?" I cut in yet again.

"I annoyed them. I thwarted them at every turn. I got in their way. So they followed me around, they investigated me, they targeted me, and in the end they found that at worst I was some kind of nut who just kept representing this convict and helping him in his—from their standpoint—strange and not well-founded actions. They found no crimes, so they made them up."

I had not yet told Sheila about my conversation with Sheffield. Now I brought it up. I told her that Sheffield had seen Bailes after his release from prison and had reproached him for "what you did to Sheila McGough."

"What did Bobby say?" Sheila asked.

"He said, 'What did I do? I didn't do anything,' and Sheffield said, 'You know what you did.' And now I come to something Bailes said that I find it very hard to repeat to you. I know you like this man so much."

"Oh, that's all right. I just felt bad that I wasn't able to solve his problems. I'm sorry it turned out the way it did for him."

I went on, "According to Sheffield, Bailes said something not nice and not true about you. He said that he hadn't done anything wrong—and that you got greedy."

"Oh, dear. Well, there are two possibilities: One is that that isn't really what Bobby said. But secondly—let me put it this way: The attorney-client relationship puts a lot of duties and restrictions on the attorney. It puts very few on the client. Everything flows in one direction. Loyalty flows only from the attorney to the client. The client is like a patient. Sometimes clients say things to protect themselves that aren't true and aren't fair. So what? It doesn't mean that you abandon them— even in your own mind."

"You're right. It's possible he didn't actually say it."

"But it doesn't matter. If he said every word, and more and worse, it wouldn't change my opinion particularly."

"But lawyers are also human beings. They have feelings."

"Oh, yes. I felt very sad when I found out Bobby died. It was a shock. I was saddened, and it was a genuine sadness. I wasn't just thinking how will this affect my situation. I'm sorry he died."

"That's why I felt bad about telling you what Sheffield said."

"That wasn't a shock. I don't know how to explain it exactly. I keep coming back to the medical analogy."

"Did you and Bailes ever talk about your trial and conviction?"

"Oh, yes. He was very sad and upset, and he blamed himself. After I was out of prison, he called me at home. He was out on probation and living with his mother in Marion, Virginia—that was a condition of his probation—and we chatted back and forth. He told me about some kind of appeal he had going— Bobby always had an appeal going—and something came up about my conviction. He expressed—as he had before—his bad feelings about it. And I was able to say to him something like, 'Just don't let anybody tell you, and don't believe it yourself, that it was your fault. Lawyers are supposed to represent people who are in trouble and who are accused of crimes, and I was just doing my job for you. Just remember—don't slip over the fact—that I was framed by the prosecutors. The prosecutors are the ones who did this to me. They made up the evidence. So don't let anybody make you feel guilty.' I'm glad I got the chance to say this to him."

EVEN AS I had put off telling Sheila about my talks with Sheffield and Sergeant, so I couldn't wait to tell her of my delightful discoveries about Morris, Manfredi, and Zinke in the archives of the Manhattan and Long Island criminal courts. (Manfredi, I was able to report with special pleasure, was back in prison—Sing Sing—for a new series of forgeries and thefts.) Here again, Sheila surprised me. Instead of expressing pleasure, she began arguing. "Just because they're criminals doesn't prove that I'm not," she said.

"If your mind didn't work this way, you might never have gone to prison," I found myself retorting.

She laughed and then said, "These are people I could have represented very comfortably."

"So it makes no difference that they are bad guys?"

"Yes, it makes a difference," she had to concede. "But they weren't the ones who put me in prison. It was the people in power who did." And once again she launched into her old diatribe.

Mark Hulkower gave me greater satisfaction. During a telephone conversation with him, I mentioned Morris's disbarment (I had not yet learned of his subsequent conviction and prison sentence), and I caught him completely off balance.

"Wait—do you mean Alan Morris, the lawyer from New York?" he asked.

"Yes."

"He's been disbarred?!"

"Yes."

"Where did you hear this?" Hulkower said in a low, tense voice.

"From the Disciplinary Committee of the New York State Supreme Court."

There was a long pause on the line. Then Hulkower recovered his composure and said, "He was an attorney of good standing at the trial." True to his litigator's training of never asking a question you don't know the answer to, he pointedly didn't ask me what Morris had been disbarred for.

"He's not in good standing now," I said, enjoying my little victory. But I couldn't sustain it. My telephone conversations with Hulkower had taken the form of cross-examinations—by him of me. These conversations allowed me to experience something every journalist knows from the other side: the power of the question. When a journalist asks a subject a question he always—or almost always—gets a lengthy answer. It is a rare person who can withstand the aggressiveness and seductiveness of a question, who can give the laconic yes, no, or I don't remember that witnesses are advised by their attorneys to limit themselves to at depositions. The normal person will respond to the built-in demand and come-on of the question by a kind of obedient babbling. When Hulkower had fully recovered from the blow of Morris's disbarment, he resumed his interrogator's role, and I resumed mine of the long-winded and placating examinee. This was Hulkower's craft, and he was very, very good at it. I was only an amateur—you don't need to be anything more to be a journalistic interviewer. You're not playing for the high stakes that litigators play for. You don't know what the answers are, and you have no wishes as to what they will be. You are only pushing a button, turning on a tap. Hulkower's questions were framed to drive me into a corner, to force me to make concessions, to oblige me to say, "Yes, I guess you're right." "I guess I can't defend this point." "No, I can't get around that." After hanging up, I always felt angry with myself for talking too much and being too conciliatory.

I once asked Sheila what she thought of Hulkower, and she said, "The only criticism I have of Mark Hulkower is that he's dishonest." She went on, "He's dynamic, intelligent, fearless—absolutely fearless. And I mean not just his demeanor. I mean that knowing what he did and what he had to lose if he was caught, he was like a bank robber."

Sheila has never been able to demonstrate to me that Hulkower and his boss, Henry Hudson, knew she was innocent and prosecuted her all the same. "I can't prove it yet," she wrote in 1996, and she hasn't proved it two years later. While it seems clear to me that Morris and Manfredi and Boccagna testified falsely when they said that Sheila told them she would hold the money in escrow, it isn't at all clear that Hulkower knew this and was cynically supporting a theory he didn't believe in. I think he believed Sheila was Bailes's gun moll and had lied and cheated on his behalf. He had never met Sheila—he didn't know what I know about her character. He professed to find my defense of her pitiful.

"I never caught Sheila in any lie," I said to Hulkower during one of my losing debates with him.

"I'm not saying she lies today," he said. "I have no notion of where she is and what she is doing."

"She wasn't caught in any lies at the trial, either. It was her word against that of other people."

"She wasn't caught in any lies because she didn't testify," Hulkower pointed out. He had me once again, of course. I had no answer.

IF MARK Hulkower is the villain of this piece, then Gary Kohlman is its antihero. He is the champion who did not rescue the maiden but left her chained to a rock on a cliff over-

looking an abyss. Kohlman was not eager to speak with me and
agreed to do so with reluctance. Like Hulkower, he understood
the stylized nature of journalistic narratives and could foresee
that his role as the lawyer who lost Sheila's case would bring
him no glory. When I called on him in his office in a large
Washington law firm, I was immediately aware that this was not
someone who thought of himself as a loser—quite the contrary.
Kohlman is a tall, elegant, well-spoken man with a gray mustache and gray hair, possessed of the sort of savoir faire that
puts every interlocutor's sense of his own social worth in doubt.
During our brief talk—he told me he could speak for only
twenty minutes because of the press of work on a case he was
trying for the Steelworkers Union against United Steel—he
subtly undermined Sheila. It seems almost humanly impossible
for a lawyer who has lost a case not to (at least in some part)
blame the client for the defeat. Sheila's blaming of herself for
losing Bailes's bank fraud and Social Security case is a bizarre
anomaly, its strangeness only heightened by the clear signs of
Bailes's guilt and the improbability of any other outcome.
When she herself was prosecuted, there is less reason to be sure
that the outcome was inevitable—that it might not have been
different if her lawyers had fought harder and been better prepared. In my study of the case, I have become aware of the soft
spots in Hulkower's argument, which Kohlman and Rochon
might have probed and didn't. I have noted numerous lapses in
their defense, such as their failure to bear down on the contra-
dictions between the deposition and trial testimony of Manfredi, Boccagna, Morris, and MacDonald and to exploit the
enormous exculpatory potential of the one-minute phone call
by Morris.

Kohlman himself, however, expressed no doubts about his
performance. He was like a surgeon looking back on an operation that failed not because of any errors on his part but because
of the necrosis he had found on making his incision. "We put
our heart and soul into this case. We pulled out all the stops,"

he said. But Sheila couldn't be saved. "She was committed to not testifying. She believed that she couldn't testify without saying something possibly derogatory or negative about her client, Mr. Bailes. This meant that we had to try the case without the testimony of the person whom the jury most wanted to hear from, the most logical person to be telling her story." He went on, "Most people would have said of Bailes, 'He's a rascal, he's had many opportunities in the criminal justice system, he doesn't deserve a further break.' Sheila personifies the passionate and idealistic lawyer who is not going to let any of that thinking color her willingness to represent her client. And that's fine. Her problems began when Bailes asked her to do things for him that started stretching the boundaries—or perhaps went beyond the boundaries—of what was necessary in representing him in his criminal case."

As Kohlman spoke, I heard the echo of Hulkower's dire opening comments about Sheila as an attorney "who crosses the line from representation of the criminal to participation in his crimes." Hadn't Kohlman himself now strayed across the line separating loyalty tempered by honesty from careless betrayal? During my conversation with him, and in certain of his remarks during Sheila's trial, Kohlman sharpened my sense of the norm of self-protective lawyerly behavior from which Sheila had so magnificently and disastrously deviated. The normal lawyer is an ambitious man or woman whose first loyalty is to his or her own career. He or she is bound by the conformist pressures every professional organization exerts on its members—none, perhaps, so acutely and overtly as the legal profession, with its hierarchy leading from puny law students to all-powerful judges. Lawyers are, for good reason, afraid of judges, and they will do almost anything to stay in their favor. Clients come and go, but judges go on forever. Thus in every trial a little drama is played out, side by side with the big one—the drama of propitiation of the judge by the lawyers. Much of this secondary drama takes place during sidebar conferences, when the lawyers drop their masks of antagonism and behave like schoolboys in front of the teacher, vying for her favor and seeking to impress her with their nice behavior toward each other. But in open court, too, the stroking of the judge goes on, as, for example, in this coquettish little exchange during Sheila's trial between Kohlman and Judge Albert Bryan, Jr., after Bryan has overruled an objection by Hulkower:

> MR. KOHLMAN: Thank you, Your Honor.
> THE COURT: You don't have to thank me for ruling in your favor.
> MR. KOHLMAN: I will thank you even if you rule against me, Your Honor.
> THE COURT: It is not done as a matter of grace.
> MR. KOHLMAN: I understand that, Your Honor. I am sure I will have plenty of opportunities to thank you even when I lose.

In her talks with me, Sheila has never criticized Kohlman or Rochon. The closest she came to doing so was in a speech she made at her sentencing hearing, when she said, "It was not possible, given the disparity in resources between the government and private lawyers with a busy practice—who did the best they could and tried very hard for me—to do the kind of intensive investigation that might be done, for example, by . . . the Public Integrity Section of the Department of Justice." At that hearing, Hulkower spoke with feeling—as Bud Albright had spoken—of the "paper blizzard" and the "hundreds of hours of Court personnel time [that] were wasted wading through the paperwork," for which offense, if for no other, Sheila should receive a more severe punishment than the mandatory three years in prison.

When Sheila got up at the sentencing hearing to speak on her own behalf, she started out, bravely enough, speaking of "my deep feeling of duty—not affection, but duty—to my client," which had prevented her from testifying. "I felt that I could not ethically and properly take the stand and refute the lies that I heard as I listened to the government's case." For "it was not possible for me to put myself in the position of being interrogated under oath by the very prosecutors who had sent a target letter to my client, who had identified him in the indictment against me as co-conspirator, someone having committed, himself, according to them, very serious crimes, and subject myself to interrogation under oath about matters dealing with that client." But then, as her lawyers must have slumped further and further in their chairs, she started to ramble on about various unfairnesses inflicted on Bailes and to get into the details of a case involving someone named Courtland Traver, "who had done something which was improper with respect to property owned by one of Mr. Bailes' companies." This at the hearing that would decide whether she would go to prison! "One of Mr. Bailes' companies!" When she finished, Hulkower said, "Ms. McGough has no understanding of the criminal nature of her conduct and no remorse for her crime," and reiterated his plea for an upward departure from the sentencing guideline. The judge said, "I don't think a departure is warranted either up or down," and felt constrained to add, "Despite the defendant's protests of doing what she did in furtherance of her client's interest, the court cannot help but feel that Bailes just ruined this woman's life."

At the end of my interview with Kohlman, he referred to something he called "the incident of the two federal judges" and said, "Sheila wasn't in any way trying to be deceptive—she's not deceptive by nature, she's not dishonest by nature—but in her commitment to Bailes she pushed things to a point she never would have pushed them if her own well-being or freedom were at stake. No one expects that degree of commitment to a client, and this might have colored the recollections of the judges and the other participants in the incident who testified against her."

"The incident of the two federal judges" hinged on an elision of speech, a gap, a lacuna, in a story told by Sheila to one of the judges, Stanley S. Harris, before whom she appeared on Bailes's behalf in March 1987. On this occasion, Sheila, who ordinarily says too much, said too little and was severely punished for her terseness, which was interpreted as deviousness. It led to proceedings against her before the District of Columbia Bar and ultimately gave Hulkower yet another striking figure for his "pattern of deceit."

Hulkower had neatly divided his case against Sheila into two main parts. The first was her participation with Bailes in the "escrow scam." The second was her collaboration with Bailes in an attempt to defraud the government of nothing less than his own person—not by the conventional method of helping him to escape from prison, but by the unusual expedient of getting him out of jail during work hours. Hulkower crisply related how "in late 1986 Bob Bailes goes to jail on bank-fraud charges, and the conspiracy now enters the second phase. Up until then, Bob Bailes and Sheila McGough had devoted their efforts to selling these insurance charters, but now that Bailes is in jail for five years, the focus of the conspiracy shifts. Money becomes secondary. The goal now is to get Bob Bailes out of jail, released into the custody of Sheila McGough by hook or by crook." Hulkower went on:

> The scheme to get Bob Bailes out of jail was creative, and it went like this: working with Bailes and one of his old cell mates by the name of Ken Riley, Sheila McGough sets up a sham bankruptcy. The sham works this way: Sheila McGough and Bob Bailes would start with one company, Preferred Research, a company that Bob Bailes controlled, a company that existed on paper. They would have this company declare bankruptcy. And then ten or twelve other companies would come out of the woodwork, and they would say, "We are owed money

by Preferred Research." These would be the creditors. Together with Preferred Research—the company controlled by Bailes—all these other companies that claimed to be owed money by Preferred Research would go to the Bankruptcy Court, and they would say to the Bankruptcy Judge, "We are owed lots of money. The only way we are going to get this money from Preferred Research is if you let its president out of jail; let him out of jail so that he can gather up the books and records and protect the assets of the company. . . .

Now the Bankruptcy Judge will tell you that he never would have granted such a motion—to release a federal prisoner—if it had been brought only by Bob Bailes, or only by the company Bob Bailes controlled. But when the Bankruptcy Judge sees a lot of supposedly independent companies, represented by supposedly independent lawyers, he thinks, "Well, maybe if Bob Bailes moves to a halfway house from federal prison, all these companies can be paid the more than a million dollars they are owed."

Hulkower continued, in his clear and crisp manner, to tell the story of how the "supposedly independent companies" were actually under the control of Sheila and Bob, who had secretly hired the "supposedly independent lawyers" through Ken Riley and were paying them from funds in Sheila's trust account. He went on to tell of how the bankruptcy judge, George Bason, convinced by the show of creditors, signed an order permitting Bailes to be released to a halfway house in Washington, D.C. With Judge Bason's order in hand, Hulkower said, Sheila went to a federal district court judge, Charles Richey, to have it validated, but Richey would not do so without the approval of the United States Attorney's Office. This approval was not given. Hulkower moved in for the kill:

Now Sheila McGough knew at that point that she could not go back to Judge Richey, because Judge Richey had told her that he would not sign the order without the approval of the United States Attorney's office, so here is what Sheila McGough did: she waited until the weekend. She waited until Judge Richey was out of Court and she . . . went behind Judge Richey's back to United States District Judge Harris, and she told Judge Harris that it was an emergency. She told Judge Harris that it was a very simple matter. She didn't tell him she had been to any other judge, that Judge Richey had refused to sign it. And she falsely told Judge Harris that the United States Attorney's Office and the Bureau of Prisons did not oppose moving Bob Bailes to a halfway house. . . . Now Judge Harris, relying on this false information from Sheila McGough, signed the order and, as a result, Bob Bailes was brought down from federal prison for daily release into the custody of Sheila McGough.

In contrast to Hulkower's elegant lawyer's narrative, here is Sheila's version (as contained in a letter to a Mr. Thomas Henderson of the District of Columbia Bar), which has all the dumb discursiveness—and truthfulness—of a girl's letter from camp:

> . . . Judge Bason issued a writ to bring Mr. Bailes from Allenwood F. P. C. to a halfway house in Washington for sixty days so he could work with attorneys on a Chapter 11 case. . . . After the writ was issued, I went looking for a United States District Judge to give it his imprimatur, just in case there was any question about jurisdiction. It was late afternoon, March 12. The bankruptcy lawyer, Mitchell Singer, and I went to the office of the emergency judge on call. We were told he wasn't

available, but that Judge Richey would see us. We asked Judge Richey to "sign off" on the bankruptcy writ. He saw the name of Patricia Frohman [a representative of the United States Attorney's Office] mentioned in the order. Judge Richey said if we'd have Ms. Frohman endorse an order, he'd be glad to enter it for us.

The next day was Friday. I took an order to the United States Attorney's office in D.C. and asked Ms. Frohman to endorse it. She said she didn't understand why she should be involved, since her office did not represent the Bureau of Prisons. I urged her to endorse it anyway. I said something like, "What's the harm if it's not necessary?" She hesitated and said she thought she'd better check with her boss. Ms. Frohman and I then went to the office of John Birch, one of the senior assistants in the office. He recognized me as Bailes' attorney and said, "Oh, it's you again." I had met Mr. Birch in early January 1987. Mr. Bailes was then in Petersburg Camp in Virginia. He had made numerous written requests to have his eyes examined because he said he was losing his vision. After about two months, an optometrist looked at him and noted on his medical chart that he needed to be seen by an ophthalmologist as soon as possible. The Petersburg authorities were unwilling to schedule an examination by a medical doctor sooner than two weeks. I brought an emergency motion in United States District Court in D.C. (where the headquarters of the Bureau of Prisons is located) and asked for an order directing Petersburg to have Mr. Bailes' eyes examined by an ophthalmologist forthwith. Mr. Birch opposed the motion on behalf of the United States. I had talked with Mr. Birch by phone the night before the hearing on my motion; at that time, I gave him all the information I had and suggested he call Petersburg to see what could be worked out. The next morning I went to court in D.C. and made my argument. I said, "All we want is for Mr. Bailes to be examined promptly by a doctor specializing in disorders of the eyes because I have consulted a local physician who treats diabetics like Mr. Bailes and he said this condition could be a complication of diabetes and if not treated promptly, could lead to irreversible loss of vision." After I had finished, the judge indicated that that didn't seem an unreasonable request. Then Mr. Birch told the court that Mr. Bailes was at that moment on his way to Allenwood, Pennsylvania, where he was sure he would be well taken care of. When I asked if Mr. Bailes would be seen by an ophthalmologist that day, Mr. Birch said that would not be feasible because of the long distance and because there was a snowstorm in central Pennsylvania. I pointed out that it was clear and dry in the Petersburg-Richmond area and there were any number of ophthalmologists down there as well as a regional hospital only a few miles from the camp. Later, the medical officer at Allenwood confirmed that Mr. Bailes had suffered a major loss of vision. His eyes still have not been treated.

But I digress. On March 13, a Friday, Mr. Birch recognized me. When Ms. Frohman explained about the writ to bring Mr. Bailes to D.C. and my request for an endorsement, Mr. Birch said, "We're not transferring that schmuck anywhere." Mr. Birch's demeanor was insulting to me. After I left his office, I wrote in my pocket calendar some of the things he had said. Ms. Frohman and I left his office. She called Mr. Birch from her office and they talked for about a minute. Ms. Frohman made several calls while I waited in the reception area. At one point she let me talk on her phone to a woman who said she was with the Bureau of Prisons and who suggested that Mr. Bailes stay at the Federal Prison Camp at Petersburg, Virginia. I explained that it takes three hours to drive from Petersburg to D.C. if the traffic is light. Eventually, I went home without an endorsement on the order.

The next day, Saturday, I realized that I had missed a crucial fact: Ms. Frohman and her office had no standing in this matter. She had said so, on the record, at the hearing in bankruptcy court. That's what I should have told Judge Richey. By going to Ms. Frohman for an unnecessary endorsement, I had brought the transfer to the attention of John Birch, who obviously had developed a strong dislike for me and my client. Furthermore, the Bureau of Prisons had already taken the position that it did not oppose Mr. Bailes' transfer to Shaw No. 1 (the halfway house). The Bureau's designated representative, C. P. Paine, had appeared in court and had told the Bankruptcy Judge that there was no objection to the transfer (trans. p. 18, lines 1–21). Mr. Paine even mentioned that he had confirmed Mr. Bailes' community custody status (trans. p. 28, lines 19–20). There was no basis for an assistant United States attorney to call around the Bureau of Prisons for a "second opinion" after Judge Bason's order had been entered. So, I prepared another order, got in touch with the assistant to the judge on call (Stanley Harris) and made an appointment to bring him the order Monday morning.

On March 16, I went to Judge Harris's chambers with the attorney for the debtor company and we presented the order. We told the judge briefly about the bankruptcy hearing, but he said he had read Judge Bason's order, which gave a rather full summary of the proceedings and the reasons for granting the order of transfer. Judge Harris entered the order giving full faith and credit to the order of Judge Bason. Our meeting with him took about one minute. Judge Harris did not ask for an endorsement from anyone, and I didn't ask him to listen to the long and intricate story of Judge Richey and Patricia Frohman and John Birch's prior involvement with Bailes' case and Ms. Frohman's statement in court that she had no standing in the matter of Bailes' transfer. I just didn't think it was necessary.

But it was. Like a parent who gives a child permission to go to the movies and then learns that the other parent had expressly forbidden him to do so, Judge Harris was incensed when he learned—from John Birch—about Judge Richey's refusal. He rescinded his order and reprimanded Sheila. "I apologized to him and said if I had to do it over, I would tell him the story. That was the end of the matter as it concerned me." But four months later, Harris felt moved to complain to the Washington, D.C., Bar Association of Sheila's attempt to deceive him, and three years later he testified against her at her criminal trial.

"I can't tell you how minor this matter was at the time," Sheila said to me. But it was the multiplicity of such minor matters that gave Hulkower his case. "Forum shopping," as Sheila's "incident of the two judges" is called among lawyers, hardly merits a jail sentence, nor does, for instance, asking Linda Cooley to notarize a document by mail. But when there are so many of these incidents, a feeling of suspicion begins to arise and, finally, one of antipathy toward the person who appears to be always trying to get away with something. The mix of false and true charges against Sheila—false charges of criminality and true charges of impropriety—was a deadly combination. If there is every reason to doubt that Sheila conspired with Bailes in the $75,000 escrow matter, it is beyond dispute that she did not tell Judge Harris that Judge Richey had said no, and her lapse in the minor instance damaged her credibility in the major one. The moral of Sheila's story—one of the morals of Sheila's story—is: Listen to your mother. Do all the stupid little things she tells you to do. Never go to bed without brushing your teeth. Always wear presentable underwear in case you get run over.

When a taxi deposited me in front of the small brick house in southeast Washington that used to be the law office of Kohlman and Rochon, and where Rochon now practices with a partner named Michele Roberts, I found the front door open, and through it I could see a narrow vestibule—it put me in mind of the waiting rooms of rural veterinarians—where an elderly black couple sat with an air of patient immobility. It was an exceptionally hot day in June, and, as I was immediately aware when I stepped into the stifling house, the air-conditioning wasn't working. Beyond the vestibule, in an open office space, a black woman with short hair and dangling earrings, dressed in jeans and a white blouse, sat at a desk and greeted me pleasantly. When I gave her my name, she nodded and said that Rochon had been delayed in court but was expecting me. I took a seat in the vestibule and observed the scene in the office, which had an air of improvisation, like that of a student union, with its exposed brick wall, a poster of a Gauguin painting, and a young man and woman—white, in beige shorts and white shirts (they might have been law students)—shuffling file folders and leafing through lawbooks while they carried on an intermittent and bantering conversation with the woman at the desk. As I listened ("I don't like this statement of facts," the woman said to the young man), I realized that she was not a receptionist but a lawyer—perhaps Michele Roberts herself.

In about twenty minutes, a young white man, wearing a pin-striped suit, walked in, as if onto a stage, pointed a finger at me, stated my name, and introduced himself as Mark Rochon. He apologized for being late and said he would see me in a few minutes, as soon as he had taken care of the elderly couple, who then followed him up the steep stairs of the narrow house. A few minutes later, they came down and Rochon called for me to

come up. As I entered his office he was unconcernedly chang-
ing into a pair of beige shorts, like those of the law clerks downstairs. He put his bare feet up on his desk and motioned me to a
chair opposite. He was about ten years younger than Kohlman
and had a boyish air that made him seem even younger.

I had gathered from Sheila that of her two lawyers, Rochon
had been the one she felt more drawn to. He had visited her in
prison, and they had hugged, she said, offering this as an example of attorney-client behavior from which no bad inferences
can be drawn, while at the same time—this touched me—seem-
ing astonished and abashed by her departure from her normal
reserve. (Once, in telling me about her life as an adolescent, she
had said, "I was chaste and modest," unnecessarily adding, "I
didn't run around. I wasn't fast.") Rochon had further endeared
himself to Sheila by writing a long letter protesting her conviction to the president of the National Association of Criminal
Defense Lawyers, declaring that his client's prosecution
"threatens any zealous defense attorney willing to 'go to the
mat' for a client."

But now, like Kohlman, Rochon subtly undermined Sheila.
Even in his letter to the NACDL, he had qualified his support
of her: "The evidence at Ms. McGough's trial was *almost entirely*
acts that a lawyer could and should do for a client" (italics
mine). And now, with the same lawyerly precision, he said, "A
lot of what Sheila did is just not criminal behavior." (A lot?) He
went on, "What did she do? She simply followed the directions
of that idiot. She lacked common sense. She was brand-new out
of law school, with no supporting network of lawyers to temper
her judgment. When you lose your first trial, you go out with
other lawyers and have a drink, and they console you. You learn
how to deal with the profession. She didn't have any of that.
She's no criminal, but she could have benefited from some outside judgment. She should have been in the Public Defender's
Office. She would have been a great public defender. I am an
ex–public defender, and so is Gary Kohlman. But at the time

she was defending Bailes, there was no Public Defender's Office in Virginia. She was a solo practitioner taking court-appointed cases. That's a completely different experience. She was alone, with no one to consult. She lived with her parents, led a sheltered life. Then she was thrown into the maelstrom of criminal defense. It's a recipe for disaster.

"The U.S. Attorney's Office in Alexandria goes after lawyers. It's a jurisdiction unlike any other in this country. There's no place like the Eastern District of Virginia. There's no place else in the country where a Sheila McGough would get prosecuted. Moreover, the Eastern District has one of the highest conviction rates in the country. Jurors are drawn from a class that works in government and defense and related industries. They are tough jurors. A tough, tough, tough crowd. I know many lawyers who prefer not to practice in the Eastern District because of that.

"That poor woman shouldn't have been prosecuted. In any reasonable world, she would have learned that you can't do these things. She might have been referred for bar counseling to see if she had made mistakes. But what she did was not a crime. It's hard for me to figure her out entirely, because she's a very different person than I am. Her life experiences are dramatically different from mine. I once had dinner with her and her parents at a steak house called the Ponderosa, which is a fine restaurant, but sitting there with them, I got such a strong sense of small-town America. Here is this trusting, naive, stay-at-home spinster type—who knows about the steak specials at Ponderosa so that she and her family can go out on those nights and eat more cheaply—practicing law in the cesspool of the criminal defense world, amidst the lavish lifestyle and rip-and-run mentality of young Washington lawyers.

"She thought being innocent was a defense—as opposed to establishing a reasonable doubt in some jurors' minds. I don't care what the reasonable doubt is if it will win and if you don't break laws to establish it. From a lawyer's point of view, being innocent is meaningless. I say this to my clients all the time. They tell me what happened, and I say, 'I don't give a flying whatever what happened, because you're not going to testify and say what happened. You've got a record, and if you testify, that record will come in. So what happened doesn't matter anymore.' "

"But Sheila didn't have a record."

"I know. But if she had testified, what would she have said? She would have said that Bailes was innocent and wrongly accused. That he was the victim of a vicious prosecution. That the charters were valid."

"So you don't agree with Kohlman that Sheila should have testified?"

"I don't. Look, you always regret losing at trial. But with a perfectly malleable client, it's easier to win. And by malleable, I don't mean one who is going to lie. I mean one who can be sat down and read the riot act to about what the truth is."

"You mean what the story you want to tell is."

"Right. Since who knows what the truth is."

"But there are some things you *know* are true. You know whether you talked to someone on the phone and promised him an escrow agreement—or you didn't."

Rochon was not interested in my point. "Yes, but the larger problem is this: Suppose the story your client wants you to tell the jury is that Bailes is a complete innocent. That the charters are real. That she wasn't duped. That Bob Bailes and she are both victims of the government. If your client tells you this, is it wrong to convince her that that's a crock of shit? A lawyer who could have stood up in court and said, 'Bob Bailes is a scumbag and he's used this poor woman for all she was worth and took advantage of her principles'—that lawyer would have had a pretty good shot at winning this trial, even with an Eastern District jury. But Sheila would never have countenanced that. That was the real tension of the trial—her undying loyalty to her client, her insistence that his interests be zealously protected throughout the proceedings. This tied our hands—and this, ultimately, is why the law was probably the wrong line of work for her."

Rochon paused to take a telephone call (he made an arrangement to meet someone at a restaurant with a French name and did not inquire about the specials), and when he had finished, I asked if the woman downstairs was Michele Roberts. "The casually dressed woman at the desk? Yes. Half my clients come in and think she must be the secretary. She dupes them and then gets mad at them for assuming she's a secretary—because she's a woman and she's black and she's dressed like a bum."

Returning to Sheila's trial, I mentioned Hulkower, and Rochon said, "He had a very self-righteous attitude as a prosecutor, so I think it's ironic—deliciously ironic—that he's now in private practice representing child-molesters." Rochon was referring, I later learned, to Hulkower's representation of the Nobel Prize scientist Daniel Carleton Gajdusek, who had been indicted for sexually abusing a Micronesian boy he picked up on a research expedition and brought back to America; Hulkower arranged a plea bargain for him of one year in prison instead of the thirty years he risked by going to trial. Rochon added, "When you consider the things a defense attorney has to do for his clients, it's possible that Mr. Hulkower may be doing the things he damned Sheila for doing."

Rochon's deepest antipathy, however, was reserved for Kirkpatrick MacDonald. "I've always felt there was something I didn't find out about him that could have helped to pull this case apart. I've got very good instincts—I really do. I can spot a liar or a fraud. I would probably be a good poker player if I cared about poker. And there was more to that guy than came out on the stand. The hostility he had went way beyond the bounds. The guy didn't lose any money. There was a potential loss, but it was retrieved. His hostility went way beyond normal. When I saw him, I had a very visceral reaction. I've come to be pretty trusting of these reactions. And when I've had a chance to check them out, I've usually found there was something amiss."

ONCE DURING a telephone conversation with Sheila I was roused from my customary state of torpor and annoyance by an astonishing answer she gave to a question I had asked about her dealings with Fred Quarles, the Charlottesville money broker for whom Bailes's insurance scam was "just an interesting deal." Quarles himself had filled me with wonder when I called him a few months earlier and he affably and cheerfully recalled his disastrous adventures in the world where "you make money because you have found out something that is not common knowledge." "Bailes was just one of my adventures in 1986," he said. "Nineteen eighty-six was a memorable year. It was like a fine wine; I'm still trying to unravel a complicated fraud somebody else worked on me that year. I wasn't sure what had happened. For a long time, I thought that maybe I had screwed up. But now that I have tracked down all the documents and tied up the loose ends, I know exactly what happened. I know I got swindled. The money brokerage business is the most hazardous business I know. You're going to get clobbered. I can count on my fingers and toes all the people I've dealt with who have gone to jail. During the savings-and-loan crisis, I kept a lot of banks afloat, and then a lot of bankers went to jail. I have stopped reading the ads in the *Wall Street Journal.* I once picked four ads at random, and eventually four out of the four men who took out the ads went to prison. I decided I didn't have the qualifications for this work. I am now in a new business. I find missing people. I'm not an investigator—I just find missing people. I found a man who had disappeared with the KGB in 1939 and had died in 1947. People do strange things to make a living. It's a harsh world. God put everybody on this earth for some reason, but we don't know what it is."

In his youth, Quarles told me (he is now fifty-seven), he had been a pilot and a flying instructor (he intended to become an airline pilot but had walked out of his interview with United Airlines and taken a job flying new planes from factories), and had indulged his taste for being swindled by answering ads in treasure-hunting magazines. He related a fantastical, though vaguely familiar, story about a gold cross given to a Mexican peon by the grateful family of a Castilian aristocrat the peon had helped escape from Devil's Island, which led to the discovery of a Spanish ship wrecked off the coast of Mexico; and he recalled a visit to a treasure hunter in Texas, who had already taken three thousand dollars off him in an oil-well deal that foundered ("No oil—sorry about that. We'll get you in on the next one") and who "showed me emeralds as big as golf balls and photographs of himself standing waist-high in gold bars in a Mexican gold mine, with a pistol on his hip and a little Indian girl at his side."

Quarles had answered Bailes's *Wall Street Journal* ad of June 13, 1986, and had got sufficiently involved in the insurance scam to become an object of interest to Hulkower, who brought him before the grand jury that presently indicted Sheila. After examining Quarles, Hulkower wisely dropped him from his beak. He did not call him as a government witness at Sheila's trial. Doubtless he recognized in him a quality that made him a useless, even dangerous, witness: the quality of disinterestedness, from which no narrative good can come. Quarles lived in a world of his own and had no scores to settle; in his grand jury appearance he stubbornly ignored Hulkower's cues and perversely declined to play the role of the victim of a con artist. Kohlman and Rochon unwisely called Quarles as a defense witness and learned too late that he wouldn't play their game, either. "I don't know that I have ever come to any conclusion about what's going on here, sir," Quarles maddeningly testified during Rochon's examination. "I'm sorry, but I have looked at this and looked at it and looked at it in a hundred different ways, and I still don't know what is going on." Worse yet for Sheila, under Hulkower's cross-examination, Quarles made a damaging concession about Sheila's deceitfulness:

Q: And you asked Ms. McGough point-blank whether anything had happened to Bob Bailes within the past two weeks, correct?

A: That's correct.

Q: And she did not tell you that two weeks earlier Bob Bailes had been convicted of bank fraud in the Eastern District of Virginia with Sheila McGough representing him?

A: That's correct. The first time I learned of that was in your office.

Q: That's something you would have wanted to know, though, correct?

A: Yes. That's why I asked her.

My question to Sheila had been about this testimony. Why hadn't Rochon, when his turn came, done anything to repair the damage? Surely Hulkower was again twisting some innocent actuality to propel his dire narrative?

"Quarles told the truth. I did mislead him," Sheila said.

"What did you say!"

"Yes, I told Quarles that nothing was final, that things were on appeal. That wasn't truthful. I did try to mislead him. All I can say in my defense is that I didn't want to give out damaging information about a client without his permission. A more experienced attorney would have found a better way of doing this. I didn't do it well. He took me by surprise, and instead of a generic, lawyerlike answer like, 'Oh, I don't ever give out information about a client,' I misled him. I wasn't under oath. It wasn't illegal. But I should have done it differently."

As I listened to this speech, I felt as if the ground were giving way under me. Until this moment, it had never occurred to me to doubt the truth of anything Sheila said. She was my lodestar. Veracity was her defining characteristic, like the color of an orange. Her behavior may have been odd, deviant, maddening, but her devotion to the truth—almost like a disease in its helpless literalness—was an inspiriting given. Now I had to face the possibility, perhaps the probability, that she was the clever liar of Hulkower's narrative, and that I was a naive fool. If she could lie to Quarles, she could lie to me. No doubt she *had* lied to me. The flame of doubt began to rise and flare in my imagination. Then it sputtered and went out. Her confession to me that she had misled Quarles was only further evidence of her honesty. She could have fudged or equivocated, but she had chosen to tell the shameful truth about herself.

I have dwelled at such length on my reaction to Sheila's confession not only because it was such an extraordinary moment in my encounter with her but also because it helped me to understand something that had puzzled me about Quarles. In a letter of August 29, 1986, following up a telephone conversation he had had with Bud Albright, of the U.S. Attorney's Office in Alexandria, Quarles set forth his growing suspicion of Bailes and enclosed copies of the documents Bailes had sent him. Among these was an impressive-looking order issued by the United States District Court of Delaware, dated February 5, 1914, which stated that certain insurance companies (the ones that Bailes was now peddling) were " 'grandfathered' insurance corporations," and were "not in any way subject to regulation by any insurance department, commissioner or any other official of any state, territory or by the District of Columbia." "According to my attorney, Robert Musselman, of Charlottesville," Quarles wrote Albright, "this is not possible, because the Circuit Court System was abolished by an act of Congress on 3-3-1911, which became effective 1-1-1912. Thus on the face of it, this could be construed as fraudulent. Indeed," he went on to write, "[it] suggests that this whole thing is a fiction."

However, five days later, on September 3, after meeting with Bailes in the Roanoke airport, Quarles wrote himself a long aide-mémoire (introduced as evidence in Sheila's trial), indicating that he had rid himself of his doubts and was back among the believers in Bailes's interesting deal. His unwillingness to change his mind about Bailes—like my unwillingness to change my mind about Sheila—overcame the pressures on him to do so. The contest is such an unequal one—the force with which we cling to our opinions is such a strong one—that a volte-face is a rare and extraordinary event that takes place only when the evidence that we are wrong beats us down like a powerful surf. We maintain a loyalty to our opinions that is like our loyalty to friends; to change our minds seems a kind of betrayal. As nothing will now shake my faith in Sheila, so nothing will convince Hulkower that he was wrong to prosecute her. When a jury begins to deliberate, its members are similarly stuck in the mire of their preconceptions. The jury system is posited on the idea that people are capable of suspending their normal state of having a fixed opinion about everything and allowing new ideas to penetrate the defenses of their old ones. But this is like believing people capable of suspending the peristaltic motion of their stomachs. It is like imagining a ballpark filled with placidly neutral spectators. Every juror listens to the testimony through the filter of his preconceptions and as a (conscious or unconscious) rooter for one side or the other. The recognition of this actuality is what gives jury selection its tense atmosphere and has, in our culture of store-bought horse sense, created an industry of experts on jury selection, to whom each side now runs for help whenever it can afford to do so.

But then, if jurors are so unalterably fixed in their preconceptions, why do trial lawyers even bother to mount a convincing case? What is the point of trying to persuade the unpersuadable? And indeed, when trial lawyers lose a case, they almost invariably cite the composition of the jury as a reason— "With that jury, what else could you expect?" (The winner, of

course, is only confirmed in his touching faith in the jury system.) In the heat of battle—while the case is still being
argued—trial attorneys are evidently able to suspend their disbelief in the idea of the open mind and address the jurors as if
they were speaking to people who are in a condition of healthy
doubt about what they think, instead of in a chronic condition
of complacent certainty. If jurors can be swayed, it is apt to be
not by trial attorneys but by other jurors during deliberations—
by the workings of group psychology, the power of strong per-
sonalities over weak ones, the pull of life outside the jury room.
But some jurors, of course, cannot be swayed. Thus, Quarles,
like the holdout against whom the eleven others finally have to
acknowledge their helplessness, stubbornly held on to his belief
in the man everyone else considered a rogue. In his long aide-
mémoire, he was able to write without irony not only of Bailes's
excuse for being an hour and a half late for his meeting in the
Roanoke airport ("On the way over, a barrel of nails had fallen
off a truck in front of him and had caused him a flat tire, and he
had had to have his car towed in") but of Bailes's explanation of
"the problems he was having with the law." There was one old
court case, Bailes said, that had been remanded for retrial, and
he expected to have it overturned shortly. "In this case,"
Quarles wrote, "he said that a banker who co-owned a bank
with him had forged his signature 292 times. . . . I asked him if
he had had any other problems with the law, and he said that
there was currently a case that he was awaiting sentencing on.
He said there was a mixup on the way his name was spelled, that
his true name was Bobby Eugene Bailes, and they had him
mixed up with a Robert Eugene Bailes. That they would not
believe his birth certificate and for that reason had charged him
with using a false Social Security number."

Bailes had brought a stack of documents bearing court seals
and clerks' signatures to the airport meeting, and Quarles, now
persuaded of the silliness of the charges against him, scrutinized them carefully (though "I was having a hard time focus-

ing my eyes because my glasses needed new prescriptions") and found nothing amiss. Presently, "I asked him about the fact that Bob Musselman had said the United States Circuit Court System was abolished on January 1, 1912, by an act of Congress on March 3, 1911." Without missing a beat, Bailes said that he had "asked his attorney about that, and that he had been advised that the three circuit courts were abolished July 1, 1939, when the Federal District Courts were established." At the close of the meeting, Quarles notes, "I offered to take him back to his car, but he said he would catch a cab." Eight months later, Quarles was still attempting to broker deals between Bailes and prospective investors. On May 14, 1987, in a letter to one of them, a man named Rus Levin, he wrote, "Rus, I have spent over a year with this deal, and although it is 'strange,' I believe it is a once-in-a-lifetime opportunity that is impossible to duplicate. It's a multi-billion dollar opportunity being offered, if you want to pursue it."

When I spoke with Quarles on the telephone, I told him that Bailes had died, and he said, "I'm sorry he's dead. He was an easygoing guy. Very affable. You asked him a question and he would have an answer. Sometimes different, but plausible. Very easygoing. It seemed likely that what he was saying was true—and we could make some money off it. The insurance industry was afraid that Bailes had come up with some aberration in the system that would effectively wipe them out. They did everything they could to stop him. It seemed like Bailes had come across this aberration, and I was able to independently corroborate it with a gentleman I know who is some seventy years old. He said he had heard of it. He didn't have any documents, but he had heard of it twenty or thirty years before. He'd been in the financial business for many, many years, and he's someone I place a lot of confidence in, because he's been in the business long enough to have seen all the scams and have run into all the players. When I need a contact anywhere in the world, he's the guy I call. He makes one or two telephone calls, and the next thing I know, I'm talking to somebody that's a major world player. So when I asked him about it, he said, 'Yeah, I seem to remember hearing about these old insurance charters. They seem to surface every now and then. The legal system always pooh-poohs it, because it's not something they understand and they're afraid of it.' And I said to myself, 'I'm certainly not afraid of it. I want to know enough about it to determine whether it's real or not.'

"Bailes said he would give me the option to buy the last one. And we had people who were saying they would pay the purchase price and pick up a couple- or three-million-dollar profit. Bailes wanted only one million. People were calling in. Just standing in line. You know, going crazy to get in on the deal. I'm sitting there thinking this is a pretty ridiculous story. But on the other hand, I told the people, 'If you want to buy, I'll answer your questions as best I can, but you're free, white, and twenty-one. If you want to buy it, we'll take your money.' "

I asked Quarles what had finally frightened off the people standing in line; he had evidently not consummated a deal with anyone.

"I think it's because the insurance industry came down on Bailes so hard. They brought in his criminal record. He is dead now, and the official record is that he was a con man. He had been convicted of a lot of things before I met him, and when I asked him about some of them, he said, 'The problem with the Social Security number and the wrong name was because my family was a bunch of hillbillies and didn't know how to spell their names.' Well, I've seen situations like that. I've seen the government do things that are just corrupt. Do I think they did them to Bailes? I don't know. The biggest question in my mind is why is it that a court can't produce documents that the court clerk said she signed? Why is the file with these documents missing?"

The documents Quarles was referring to were the orders from the abolished Delaware court, which, however, he had

persuaded himself were authentic. To further satisfy himself of
their authenticity, Quarles telephoned the district court in
Washington, D.C. (to which Bailes had taken them for authen-
tication, he said), and was able to find the clerk, Karen Keyes,
whose signature and seal appeared on the cover of Bailes's documents, certifying that they were true copies of the originals.
She said yes, she vaguely remembered them. But when Quarles
called again, to order further certified copies, he was told that
the originals had disappeared. "Karen Keyes said, 'We can't
find them. We have torn the place apart and can't find the
folder for the orders.' When I told Bailes this, he said the folder
was no longer there because the Justice Department had taken
it away. Would the Justice Department do something like that?
What do you think? Why is it that a United States court can't
find the file? Why is it that a United States senator, Senator
Warner, who I called, can't get a copy of a file that is kept under
lock and key in a United States court? Who would have access
to it? Certainly the United States Justice Department. Certainly the United States Justice Department has an interest in
nailing Bailes. Certainly the United States Justice Department
has been accused in the past of withholding evidence that
would clear somebody. For me, it all came back to the fact that
Bailes had a handwritten document that was authenticated by
the court. And once that sort of thing is authenticated by the
court, it becomes real—whether it's real or not."

IN THE fall of 1996, I flew down to Florida to speak with
Debra Stuart, the federal prosecutor who had represented the
government at Bailes's 1988 trial in Charlotte for the insurance
charter scam, at which he had represented himself; she now
works in the civil section of the United States Attorney's Office
in Miami, with quarters in a huge new building of rather
aggressive nondescriptness. Stuart is a handsome, heavyset
woman in her late forties, with an easy, friendly manner and a

deep-throated laugh. When I told her that Bailes had died, she, like Quarles, expressed immediate regret. "I'll never forget Mr. Bailes," she said. "He was a character. When we were waiting for the jury to return with a verdict, he came over to me and gave me this big smile and said, 'Miss Stuart, you're the meanest woman in Charlotte.'" She laughed and added, "It was a kind of mischievous smile. He was a character. I'm sorry he's gone."

I asked Stuart what she had thought of Bailes's performance as his own advocate. "It's never a good idea to be your own lawyer," she said, "but he didn't do too badly, considering." I was surprised to hear Stuart say that. In my reading of the transcript of the Charlotte trial, I thought Bailes had done extremely badly. His defense of himself had seemed to me hopeless and pathetic. His cross-examinations had gone nowhere; they simply filled up time or gave adverse witnesses the chance to deliver their punishing blows a second time. Stuart herself, in contrast, worked with beautiful precision and economy. She was like a neat seamstress or an accurate carpenter. Perhaps her natural caution had caused her to overestimate Bailes's abilities, though Bailes's magnetism—his con artist's mesmerizing self-confidence—doubtless also played a role in brushing what, in cold print, is simply ludicrous and pitiful with the illusion of effectiveness.

I asked Stuart if she had had any doubt about what the verdict would be.

"We felt like our case was strong," she said. "But in a white-collar case you're never sure, because sometimes the jury can get confused. They can look at the thing and say, 'We don't really understand it, and we're not going to convict.'"

Stuart herself had not understood it at first. In her closing statement to the jury, she said, "The way Mr. Bailes operates, it's so convoluted, it really takes more than one person to figure out what he's doing, and even experts are temporarily fooled," adding, "You have to take five days of court time and all the witnesses that have been brought here and the public officials of twelve states, all together in one room, to get the evidence out." In 1986, when Bud Albright was whimpering about the homework he had had to do to convict Bailes of bank fraud, Stuart had already put in two years preparing her case of "Scheme and Artifice to Defraud," and two more years of work lay ahead of her. She had first set foot in the vine-choked wastes of the insurance charter scam in the summer of 1984, when FBI agents, armed with a search warrant, raided the office that Bailes was then renting on the outskirts of Charlotte and deposited a truckful of documents in her office. The raid had been set in motion by two telephone calls the FBI received—one from a midwestern lawyer named William Paul Brady and the other from a Charlotte insurance agent named Eugene Goldberg. Four years later, both men were called by the government to testify against Bailes, and they did so with evident relish. Brady appeared on the first day of trial and said that he had flown down to Charlotte in June 1984 as the emissary of a medical insurance company in Minneapolis to give Bailes a check for ten thousand dollars as an option payment on one of the unregulated insurance companies, which had been advertised, as usual, in the *Wall Street Journal* and was priced at one million dollars. Brady was skeptical from the start, but his boss ("a very big man and kind of an aggressive guy") said to him, " 'Now when you go down there . . . don't start thinking like an attorney and screw the deal up. Just give them the check and get the option agreement signed and come home.' So that was my charge."

Brady met with Bailes in the lobby of Brady's hotel. Bailes, Brady said, was "well dressed, in a tan business suit, blue shirt, nice tie, holding a manila folder in his hand, and . . . he greeted me and shook my hand the way I would enter into any meeting with anybody." The two men sat down at a little table in the lobby, and Bailes "slid this manila folder over to me." Inside were three copies of the option agreement. Brady read the agreement, and when he had finished, Bailes casually said, "If you're satisfied, why don't you just go ahead and sign it and give me the check, and we'll get going on this." But Brady did not open his briefcase and take out the check. Instead, he inquired about a woman named Rebecca Staples, whose signature appeared at the bottom of the option agreement, above the title "Trustee of the United States Hall of Fame Foundation."

That con artists are indeed artists rather than mere journeymen (like burglars) is demonstrated by their love of invention and dislike of repetition. An artist by definition is someone who refuses to repeat himself, and the con artist, accordingly, keeps introducing variations into his scam to prevent it from becoming a piece of stale and mechanical hackwork. The United States Hall of Fame Foundation was one such variation. Bailes represented it to be the metaorganization that controlled not only the insurance companies but such lesser halls as the Hall of Golf, the Hall of Baseball, and the Hall of Football. As for his own role in the deal, he said, he was a broker in a firm called First American Business Brokers and was simply acting as a middleman.

"Where does Rebecca Staples live?" Brady said he asked, as if his boss had never told him to "just give them the check." When Bailes said that Staples lived right there in Charlotte, Brady asked to meet her, and Bailes obligingly went off to fetch her.

While Bailes was away, Brady used the time to go to his room and make telephone calls, from which he learned that there was no such company as First American Business Brokers anywhere in North Carolina, nor was there anyone named Bailes who was licensed to act as a broker. He then called his boss in Minneapolis (to whom he would presently say that "if he wanted to come down and throw his money out the window he was certainly welcome to do that, but I didn't think he could expect me to do that on his behalf"), and while he was "on hold," there was a knock on his door. It was Bailes. He had been trying to call Brady from the lobby and, not being able to get through, had come up to let him know that he and Rebecca Staples were in the hotel. "We're here," Brady said Bailes said.

Brady is the kind of witness trial lawyers treasure beyond all others. His account is full of the small, everyday, random-seeming actions through which the fiction style called realism renders its powerful illusion of truth, and whose effect on juries is similarly potent. As the realist novelist uses these slight, unremarkable movements of life as hooks for securing the reader's belief in the large, more extraordinary events of his narrative, so the realist trial witness offers prosaic details (like the knock on the door) as tokens of his veracity.

Brady told Bailes he'd be "right down after I finish my telephone conversation." He had decided—perhaps looking ahead to the telephone call he would make to the FBI—to string Bailes along. He went down and chatted with Bailes and Rebecca Staples in the lobby. He asked Staples some questions about the Hall of Fame Foundation and perused another document Bailes had produced, which gave Bailes authority to sell the insurance company under discussion for the United States Hall of Fame Foundation. This document was signed for the foundation by a David Bubar.

"Who's Mr. Bubar?" Brady asked, and Bailes said that he, too, was a trustee.

"I said, 'Well, where is Mr. Bubar?' " Brady's testimony continues, "and he said, 'Mr. Bubar is in Albany, New York.' "

Brady asked Bailes if they might dine together, but Bailes "indicated that he wouldn't have an opportunity, because he was closing on a truck stop that he was selling that evening, and he'd be tied up all night." Brady then asked Staples if she was free for dinner. At this, Staples "looked a little panicked," but "Bailes jumped back in and said, 'Well, Ms. Staples' brother, who is a professor at New York University, is flying into town because their mother is very sick and she's at a beach house on the coast spending her last days.' She was dying, they indicated. So Mr. Bailes had to rush Ms. Staples out to the airport to pick up her brother, the professor, and they were then going to continue . . . to the beach house and her sick mother."

That evening, Brady looked up Rebecca Staples in the Charlotte phone book, found her listed, and sadistically called her. "Of course, she was very surprised that I was on the line because she was supposed to be at the beach house," he testified. Brady, continuing to be the innocent dupe, let her off the hook and said he had just called to confirm an appointment he had made with Bailes for the next morning to consummate the deal. He also called the other trustee, David Bubar, in Albany. "I began by telling him the facts that had been told to me, that Mr. Bailes . . . had authority to sell this company," he testified. "And he said, 'That's right,' and I said, 'And the company is licensed in all fifty states?' and he said, 'That's right.' Then I started adding some more facts that had been given to me from Mr. Bailes, and after I had him agreeing with everything, I started making facts up to which he agreed 'that's right.' And it seemed like everything I said was 'that's right.' "

Bubar himself took the stand the next day and acknowledged that he had been put up to posing as a trustee by Bailes, an old prison pal. (Bubar had been in for arson and conspiracy.) "I told them what Bailes told me to say," he testified. "I did repeat that back to them, yes."

The prosecutor asked, "Did you have any independent knowledge of the facts you told this person?"

"No," Bubar replied, "Oh, no. No, nothing except what Mr. Bailes had told me. I knew nothing about his business affairs, nothing."

"You were just as a friendly gesture accommodating him?"

"Yes, I wanted to help him if I could." And, later in the examination: "He asked me the information—exactly what Bob said he would ask—and I gave it to him."

Goldberg testified a day later. He said he had answered Bailes's *Wall Street Journal* ad of July 12, 1984, and had met with him for lunch at Charlotte's Sheraton Hotel. Almost at once, "I knew something was wrong in Denmark," Goldberg testified.

"Did Mr. Bailes indicate to you that he personally owned 150 or 160 nursing homes?" Stuart asked Goldberg.

"Yes, he did."

"Did he also indicate to you that he even had a Morrisville, North Carolina, nursing home?"

"Yes, he did."

"And did he indicate to you that he was involved in a venture involving satellites, including the Sputnik?"

"Right, he did."

"What was your response when he began to tell you about his other businesses?"

"Well, I would ask inquisitive questions, but I already had a sincere doubt, because a man who flies around in his own jet plane would at least have somebody shine his shoes. His were not clean."

Goldberg went on to testify about the aftermath of his call to the FBI. He had parted from Bailes with an agreement to meet again in Goldberg's office to continue negotiations. The FBI, accordingly, sent over an undercover agent named Deborah Decker to pose as Goldberg's secretary and to make the secret recording that is the FBI's reflexive signature act. Like Brady before him, Goldberg played to the jury's sense of the absurd, as he described a farcical moment when "I heard the tape recorder click and I was quite concerned whether Mr. Bailes would hear the same thing I did and I knew that we had run out of tape at that point." The transcript continues: "I had served coffee to him. I suggested that we both go to the men's room, he probably needs it as much as I do; and as I was leaving, I notified Special Agent Decker that some equipment needs attending to back in my office as we two gentlemen went to the men's room. That gave her time to turn it over."

Agent Decker then picked up the narrative and testified about the raid on Bailes's office, made at night with the collusion of his faithless secretary, Nancy Holland, who had told Decker that two of Bailes's paychecks to her had bounced and that she had had some reservations about "what had been going on in the office." (When Holland herself testified later, Bailes, in his cross-examination, achieved a rare triumph in getting her to concede that she had been repaid for the bounced checks by Bailes's mother.) Decker described what she had seen in Bailes's office: "option agreements, bank statements, telephone toll records, letters, *Wall Street Journal* invoices, stacks of addressed envelopes which appeared as if they were about to be mailed, sample letters, marketing agreements, lists of telephone numbers and addresses, a folder on the Hall of Fame Foundation, franchise agreements, . . . a list of North Carolina nursing homes, a large attaché case full of original documents and charters, lease agreements, amendments or documents which appeared to be amendments and revised amendments to articles of incorporation for one company or another." She cited similar documents that had been plucked in endless replication from a stack of boxes in the garage.

These papers formed the government's case against Bailes. However, they did not speak for themselves in the way Bailes's unpolished shoes and Rebecca Staples's mother's beach house did. On the contrary, they so artfully resisted the government's efforts to prod them into intelligibility that Stuart, despite her four years of patient study and her summoning of court officials from twelve states, was never able to get to the bottom of her quarry's equivalent of Marianne Moore's imaginary garden with real toads in it. She could find no way to explain exactly how his bogus documents had acquired real United States Government seals and the signatures of living district court clerks. Although Stuart was able to point to such obvious lapses as a purportedly nineteenth-century document written with a

ballpoint pen and a purportedly early-twentieth-century document that listed Alaska and Hawaii as states, she could only say
that "somehow" Bailes had been able to get these things filed in
courthouses throughout the South; the court officials could
only shake their heads and lament the inadequacy of the system
against an assault of confusion as massive as that which Bailes
had visited upon it. In her closing statement, as if anticipating
Quarles's "once that sort of thing is authenticated by the court,
it becomes real—whether it's real or not," Stuart ruefully
remarked, "Once it's filed, it's filed. I mean, they [the court
clerks] can't go back and say we didn't do it." The lacunae in
Stuart's factual case didn't matter, of course. It was the impres-
sionistic testimony of Goldberg and Brady and other prospective buyers into the Hall of Fame—as well as the impression
created by the forty-odd agents and experts and bureaucrats
who grimly testified against Bailes—that determined the verdict. In no case do trials bring out the whole truth—they can
only gesture toward it—and in this case, the government's ges-
tures had the force of karate strokes. Even before Bailes entered
his defense, there was no question but that he would lose. Bailes
knew it himself, and when the government rested its devastating case, he shifted to an insanity defense and allowed a court-
appointed lawyer named James Wyatt to take over for him.
Once again, the disorder of hypercalcemia was wheeled out as
the agent of Bailes's irrepressible sociopathy. A pair of psychia-
trists was rushed to the scene to testify to his inability to think
straight. "If someone was right in their mind at that time,
would they take these charters up to experts in their field and
try to sell these insurance companies?" Wyatt unanswerably
asked in his closing statement. "I don't think anyone in their
right mind would have done what he did unless there was some
mental disease or defect that he was suffering from," he concluded. Wyatt ended his oration on a wonderful lunatic note:
"In rendering your verdict, I'm going to ask you only to do

what Euripides stated, that is, he stated, 'Unto thine own self be true and then as the night follows the day thou can be false to no one.' "

In her rebuttal statement, Stuart sneered at the insanity defense: "When Mr. Bailes first stood before you in his opening statement, he says it's all legit. But when the going gets rough, now he's crazy." She went on to say, "That is no man with cognitive defects. That man is practically a genius. It took twelve state governments and a whole squad of FBI agents to figure out what was goof-ball about the whole arrangement."

Now, sitting with me in an anonymous windowless conference room in the huge new Justice Department building in Miami, Stuart once again delivered the received wisdom about Bailes: "If only he had been able to channel that energy and intelligence into something legitimate. If he hadn't that bent in his personality, couldn't he have sold insurance? I bet he could have. He probably could have sold you a pair of dirty socks and you would have been happy." She added, "It's too bad that he died. But we all will sometime, won't we?"

Stuart's fondness for Bailes did not extend to his last advocate. When I brought up the name of Sheila McGough and said that I believed she had been unjustly prosecuted, there was a decided chill in Stuart's demeanor. The two women had never met, but they had crossed swords on paper during the year before the Charlotte trial. There had never been a question of Sheila representing Bailes at the Charlotte trial, given her idée fixe that she was to blame for the bad outcome of the fraud and Social Security trial. But with her usual fierce protectiveness, Sheila had pummeled the government with accusatory petitions and motions for Bailes that, from Stuart's standpoint, had no merit and only gave further proof of Bailes's endlessly inventive troublesomeness—now advanced through the agency of a shadowy "legal adviser." Sheila's irregular status was an affront to the correct Stuart; she judged all of Sheila's actions to be dark and unwholesome and taken in bad faith. "She had declined to make an appearance. . . . She apparently prefers to manipulate the judicial system at a distance . . . [and thus] escapes the supervision of the United States District Court for the Western District of North Carolina to hold her accountable," Stuart icily wrote in her response to a petition Sheila had filed with the United States Court of Appeals for the Fourth Circuit on the eve of the Charlotte trial.

"I can't speak to Ms. McGough's situation," Stuart said to me. "I don't know of any injustice to her. That was not my case. But I can't imagine that the prosecutor would have gone forward if he hadn't been convinced, or at least to some extent satisfied, that it was appropriate to do so. Over the years, I have seen families and girlfriends get entangled. Their hearts swell up and crowd out their brains. They're so interested in helping their brother or their boyfriend that they don't use their normal good judgment."

I said that Sheila had told me that Bailes was not her boyfriend and that I believed her.

"I can't speak to that," Stuart said again. "But let me put it this way: Let us say, as a hypothetical, that you have someone under surveillance whom you know to be a drug dealer. Let us say you have reliable information about him from informants and you follow him around, and he is always with Pedro, whoever Pedro may be. Pedro is driving him here, Pedro is driving him there, Pedro puts him to bed at night; they go to the bank, Pedro's there with him. After a while, Pedro becomes the focus of the investigation, too. It's just a natural consequence of close association."

I told Stuart a little about my acquaintance with Sheila and my sense of her as someone who could not conceivably be thought of as a criminal.

"I can see that the case troubles you," Stuart said. "When your first impression of a person is of someone who seems pretty nice, someone you'd invite to sit down with you and have a cup of coffee or to come to the garden club with you, it may seem impossible that this person would commit a crime."

"Do you belong to a garden club?" I asked. I knew that nothing I could say about Sheila would convince Stuart.

She laughed her deep laugh and said, "No. My mom did." Stuart told me that she had grown up in Greenville, South Carolina, and that her father was a retired veterinarian. She had gone to an Episcopal elementary school, to public high school, and to Duke University, from which she received both her B.A. and her law degrees. Before joining the Justice Department, she had worked for seven years in a corporate-law firm. She was around Sheila's age, and I couldn't help comparing my rash, ruined heroine with her straight-arrow, prospering counterpart, who, as it happened, had also never married and also had a small dog.

Sheila, for her part, saw Stuart as another instrument of governmental power gone out of control, and when I told her that Stuart had expressed sadness at Bailes's death, she stiffened, just as Stuart had stiffened at the mention of Sheila's name, and said, "Oh, I doubt that's true. I just don't believe it." She went on to speak—as she had spoken several times before, but she couldn't help herself—of the indignities Bailes had suffered at the hands of his persecutors. "As soon as they had indicted Bobby, they started shipping him all over the country. They put him in transit status for an entire year," she said. "He had made a fuss about something in the jail in Charlotte, and a magistrate named Barbara Delaney laid down an order that he was a troublesome, complaining prisoner: and that he was not to be held anywhere in North Carolina. So he was to be sent to a prison six hundred miles away, in Talladega, Alabama. I filed a petition against this. I said that Delaney didn't have the authority to send Bailes to a medium- or high-security prison in Alabama, that that violates his right to defend himself under the Sixth Amendment, because if he is in a maximum-security prison in Alabama, how can he get an attorney in Charlotte and prepare his defense? I lost. They kept busing Bobby around. They took this man in certifiably terrible health and bused him from place to place, so he became sicker and sicker and sicker. He almost died in Petersburg, Virginia. He had a congestive heart crisis and almost died. I went out to see him. They had hospitalized him, and here's something I saw with my own eyes—I'm not relying on something Bobby maybe exaggerated. I saw his ankles. I saw the shackles just literally cutting into his swollen ankles. It was like something you read about the way things are done in another country. I was able to get some physical relief for him there, but almost nothing else I did for him *worked*. He was the only client I ever had I couldn't seem to do anything for. Just nothing worked. Even when I knew that my legal arguments were good—that I had the facts and should prevail—*it didn't matter.* It was as if the judges had been talked to beforehand and told that I was some kind of crooked lawyer the government hadn't got quite enough evidence against yet. Only this would explain the judges' bizarre attitude toward everything I brought in. Whenever I managed to get before a fresh judge, I was treated in a very professional way and with an open mind. But the judges who dealt with me more than once or twice—I think the FBI agents who were keeping track of me and Bailes would go in and see them, and then everything changed."

For Robert D. Potter, the federal judge who presided over the Charlotte trial, Bob Bailes was hardly a fresh defendant. For over a year, Potter had been exposed to Bailes's hopelessly convoluted legal maneuverings, and in the first few minutes of the trial, in a colloquy that took place before the jury was brought in, he made his attitude toward Bailes known and set the tone that he was to maintain throughout the trial. Bailes had come into the courtroom with an announcement: "I have sarcoidosis in both eyes and both ears. I'm being treated for it, and my hearing is about forty percent; and my seeing is—goes and comes, it depends on when I put the medicine in my eyes. It's very difficult to read and very difficult to hear. I hear some things, and some things I don't. I just want it on record that I have this problem." Stuart had responded by accusing Bailes of faking: "I suggest to the court that Mr. Bailes' physical difficulties are, quote, self-imposed for the purposes of this proceeding," and had gone on to say that "the representations in the petition filed by Ms. McGough are false"—the petition said that Bailes had not been given the discovery materials to which he was entitled—and that "If he has not looked at the materials, it's been because he has not wanted to look at the materials." Bailes said reproachfully, "I don't know why she'd stand up there and say these things," and went on to make a long, incoherent speech about boxes of documents he had not been allowed to see and doctors he hadn't been allowed to subpoena to testify on his behalf. The judge then said, "Mr. Bailes, you know there's an old Aesop fable about the boy crying wolf. You've cried wolf over a year now." Bailes's response was characteristically impudent.

"I can't hear you," he said.

"What did I just say?" the judge said.

"I can't hear what you said. That's what I'm trying to say."

"All right, Mr. Bailes, you have been trying this matter for over a year. You started last August. There's an old Aesop's fable about the boy crying wolf. You've cried wolf so many times that there's no point in chasing any more rabbits. Do you understand that, sir? And I'm not going to sit here and do it."

"I don't expect you to, sir."

"All right, sir, we're going to try the case."

Midway through the trial, after a government witness whom Bailes had interminably and pointlessly cross-examined stepped down, the judge sent the jury out of the courtroom and said, "I want the record to reflect that this court has been extremely patient with this defendant, has allowed him every latitude possible. He's taken an undue amount of time for every witness that he's cross-examined with irrelevant, improper questions. I have put up with it. The United States Government has not objected to many of these questions, I guess, out of the same desire I had, to let him have every latitude he can possibly have, since he's representing himself. But there's absolutely no excuse for the time that we have spent on this case with these questions being asked by the defendant."

The judge's outburst followed one of the more farcical passages in the trial. From the transcript:

COURT: Mr. Bailes, there's twenty-five people in this courtroom waiting for you. . . . Would you move along, please, sir?

MR. BAILES: I'm trying to, sir.

*By Mr. Bailes:*

Q: Ms. Delaney—

A: Yes, Mr. Bailes.

Q: Are you a defendant in a civil lawsuit where I brought suit against you?

MS. STUART: Objection.

COURT: Objection sustained.

MR. BAILES: Well, can't I ask that?

COURT: You cannot ask that, Mr. Bailes.

MR. BAILES: Well, I'm sort of puzzled. You won't let me ask anything—

MS. STUART: I'll object to the speech of the defendant.

COURT: Sustained.

MR. BAILES: Well, I'm just trying to conduct—

COURT: Sustained, Mr. Bailes. Would you take your seat and ask a proper question? If you can't, then let's dismiss this witness.

MR. BAILES: Sir, I'm trying to ask proper questions.

COURT: Sit down.

MR. BAILES: You know I'm having a little difficulty. I don't have the papers. They won't give them to me.

COURT: Mr. Bailes, we'll have no further statements from you. If you want to ask a question, ask a question, but ask a proper question.

MR. BAILES: I have a lot of questions, but you won't let me ask them.

COURT: No, sir, I will not let you ask irrelevant, improper questions.

MR. BAILES: Well, I have a lot that's relevant and, you know, I want to try to conduct it properly.

COURT: I do not want any more statements from you, Mr. Bailes. If you have a proper question, I'll let you ask it. Otherwise I will not.

MR. BAILES: Well, how do I know whether it's proper?

As I was parting from Debra Stuart, she said again, "He was a character. I remember the trial as clearly as if it happened yesterday. I can still see the mischievous smile he gave me when he came over and said I was the meanest woman in Charlotte. I'm sorry he's gone."

WHEN FRANK Manfredi walked into the prison visiting room of Greenhaven Prison, where I awaited him one day in the winter of 1997, he looked nothing like the brutish crook of my imaginings. Gary Kohlman, in his closing statement at Sheila's criminal trial, had characterized the trio of Manfredi, Boccagna, and Morris as "that godfather crew" (which proved to be an error—it only permitted Hulkower to draw himself up later and say, "Mr. Kohlman gives you one reason why Frank Boccagna would lie, because he has an Italian surname. He and Mr. Manfredi have an Italian surname, so Mr. Kohlman calls them godfather. Come on!"), and nothing in my readings of Manfredi's criminal-court file (it included his winsome offer, when the posse was closing in, to provide the government with information about his mob connections in the carting business on Long Island) contradicted the image. So I was unprepared for the tall, slender, good-looking man with carefully cut and combed salt-and-pepper hair, wearing a stylish white sweater with an interesting collar over gray flannel trousers, who entered the room with a quiet, quick tread. He looked like a model for expensive menswear. Only when he began to speak— in the guttural tones of movie gangland—did he obligingly scurry back to his old place in my narrative.

"I responded to the ad and I spoke to the number that was there," Manfredi replied when I asked him to recall his deal with Bailes—just as he had replied in court six years earlier. "I spoke to Bailes and said I was interested in purchasing two of the insurance companies."

I opened my purse and took out the *Wall Street Journal* ad of June 13, 1986. "Was that the ad?" I asked, handing it to him.

He glanced at it and said, "Yeah."

"How did you reach Bailes through this?"

He immediately got it.

"To be blunt with you, if my life depended on it, I would have said I called a number that was in the ad. But now that I see the ad—which was never shown to me at trial—I know that I obviously wrote to them and got a response. Recollections are not strong that way."

Although his testimony had helped to convict her, Manfredi now spoke of Sheila not as an adversary but as a kind of kindred spirit. "I've been on that side with my own, you know, misuse or whatever, so I have a tremendous amount of sympathy for any attorneys who lost their licenses or had to undergo any time because of what clients did to them. I know how easy it is to get hurt by your own client. When you don't have the ability to dis-tance yourself from the client because of your own personal

makeup, your love of the battle, your caring nature for a particular client, you are subject to a fall. It happened to her, it happened to me. It happened to me twice. After I lost my license in
1985, I did a short prison term—a one-to-three. Then I tried to
get my life back together. I formed a credit service company. I
did juggle my clients' monies, but I juggled them only because I
knew full well I had access to funds. I could have written a
check and paid them in full in twenty-four hours. A lot of
people wouldn't believe that I was president of the student
organization of my law school and one of the top ten students,
and that I wrote articles that were published in various states.
But I was never able to deal with the disappointment and anger
of other people. I did not allow my clients to realize that I could
fail. I would draw them close to me. They were no longer
clients. They became friends and family, and I could not disap-
point them at any cost. If a client was losing a house and I
deflected some funds from another client, the first client was
now okay. The other client, who had the funds—that was
something I could resolve later. It was a very wrong sense of
reality. Sheila would understand exactly what I'm talking about.

"I did lose control of MacDonald and Zinke once I was
unable to, you know, pay the money. But under no circumstances did I ever suggest or want or desire anyone to go to the
prosecution against any particular attorney—my background
and where I am right now would indicate that that is not the
way I particularly work. But I was always confused as to why
Sheila allowed this particular situation to go so far, to the point
where she would face criminal charges when it was only a question of dollars. There are always ways to replace dollars. And
there is no rule of ethics that required her to go to prison to
save Bailes. Especially when he's already in prison. Wasn't it
time for her to say that maybe he's not as pristine as I antici-
pated?"

A journalistic interview is poised on the intersection of two
frequently conflicting desires: the journalist's desire to advance

a narrative, and the subject's desire to advance himself (or some enterprise that is an extension of himself). But Manfredi, the forever disbarred attorney, serving time for a second grand-larceny conviction, had no wishes for our conversation beyond its immediate use to him as a break in his dull prison day. He talked to hear himself talk; it was all nonsense; it meant nothing to him. The man was shrewd and wary and cold. My fantasy that Manfredi would break down and confess that he lied at Sheila's trial was absurd. Why should he do that? The two hours I spent with him were filled with animated talk (I kept up my end) and were as empty as the rooms of Alan Morris's old office in Garden City.

On my last train trip to Washington to see Sheila, she awaited me as usual in front of the station in her small white car. Driving to Alexandria, I said I would like to take her to lunch at an Italian restaurant I had noticed on a previous visit. It was near the building in which Sheila had once had an office—the office where she had prepared (as Linda Cooley critically watched) her defense of Bailes in the bank fraud and Social Security case, even as Bailes was reeling in Manfredi and Boccagna, and where MacDonald had secretly taped his interview with her. "Oh, that would be nice," Sheila said, adding, "I had instructions from my mom to take you to a French restaurant. She put money in my pocket." But she did not attempt to persuade me to go to the French restaurant. Some inner code of conduct—as strict as the code that had prevented her from testifying for herself at her trial—dictated that the mother's money remain in the pocket and the journalist's invitation be accepted.

As we crossed the Fourteenth Street bridge and passed the familiar monuments (as usual, the Holocaust Museum, which has settled without protest into the bland, clean landscape of the capital, had a small line of young people in front of it), Sheila told me that the three-year term of her supervised release had finally ended: she could now travel without permission, and her bedroom (and her parents' bedroom) would no longer be subject to searches by employees of the Bureau of Prisons. When I asked her something about her first days as a prisoner, in January 1991, she answered brightly, "Someday I may write a book called 'The Sensible Woman's Guide to Federal Prison.' One of my main tips will be: If the day comes when you think you might be picked up by the marshal's service, the first thing you should do—even before you call your lawyer—is to get a thick pair of socks, pull them over your ankles, and put on running shoes or sports shoes that fit comfortably and a pair of jeans, or even better, one of those sweatsuits or workout suits, made of nice soft material that you can sleep in. The reason for the socks is that marshals always shackle. If they took my mother, they would shackle her.

"When I turned myself in at the court, they put me in a holding cell. I was familiar with this. I had interviewed clients in the same cell several times. I was there all afternoon. Typically, there's an open toilet and a sink and a water fountain. There were a number of other women in the cell. Some women won't use the toilet, out of modesty. I was never like that. I come from a medical family, and you want to keep your bladder and your entire elimination system in good working order. I spent the afternoon 'in no particular distress,' as doctors would say. I just waited. In the evening, the female deputy came in and cuffed and shackled me. I was fine with it. They trucked me to a jail in Fairfax. It was very cold in the truck—they had taken away my coat."

She went on to recall other harsh prison experiences in the same uncomplaining and understated way. Predictably, however, she soon veered to the outrages that the prison authorities had committed against Bailes. But then, perhaps concerned that her own stoicism might upstage her client's, she veered again. "I speak of Bobby as a victim and pathetic figure," she said. "But he was no whiner. Though he was ill the entire time I knew him, he was habitually cheerful. He was always sick—pasty, puffy-faced, overweight. But it was only now and then that he was acutely ill. The rest of the time, he was confident and full of plans and energy. He just radiated energy. Silly as it sounds, Bobby would always try to be the good host when I came to see him in prison. He would have a nice table in the visitors' room and he'd introduce me to some of his buddies. No matter what the situation was, he was upbeat. When I lost his trial, the first thing he said was, 'Sheila, don't take on so. We'll win on appeal. You look so down-at-the-mouth, I'm going to take you out for dinner.' When I messed up the second time—when I did poorly on oral argument and he lost his appeal—I drove up to the prison and told Bobby the result, and again he was most concerned about how I felt. He said to me, 'I can do five years standing on my head. I do okay in prison. Guards like me real well.' One of his favorite expressions was: 'Well, we're just going to lose and lose until we win.' He was not treated well by the system. He was someone who needed a better lawyer than I was."

At the restaurant (as always, Sheila hardly touched her food because she had so much on her mind), she continued her self-recriminations. "I just didn't do a good job of defending Bobby in federal court. I wasn't a competent trial lawyer. I didn't know enough about federal procedure. I did everything wrong. I wasn't able to knock out their flimsy evidence. And it turned out that they had withheld important evidence—medical evidence—that would probably have led to his acquittal." The "important evidence" was a psychologist's report of January 1986, signed by Edith Breen, Ph.D.; it had been among the things impounded from Bailes's car upon his arrest in May 1986. The report—addressed "To Whom It May Concern" and written on stationery with no letterhead—spoke of injuries Bailes had suffered in two automobile accidents (one in November 1984 and the other in February 1985), which had so severely impaired his memory and generally addled his wits that "he cannot trust himself yet to write a check correctly" and has to rely on "an accountant or an attorney to handle all his business and financial affairs." Breen wrote that she had inherited Bailes from a series of other therapists, in various states, who had treated him for amnesia, confusion, depression, anxiety, post-traumatic stress disorder, headache, and inability to concentrate, among other symptoms—all of which would have explained and excused Bailes's giving of false information to the bank. If he couldn't even tell his own lawyer about the accidents (he had forgotten them!), Sheila said, still indignant, "how could he have been expected to remember what he owned and didn't own and what his Social Security number was?"

In a remarkable Motion for a Reduction of Sentence, dated August 5, 1987, Sheila set down these and a great many other reasons for the government to recognize its error and to commute the remainder of Bailes's five-year sentence to three months of house arrest. "For whatever wrongdoing he committed . . . while he was suffering from documented mental impairment, Bailes had suffered enough," the motion states. "He should be allowed to go home now, and work with his private physician to preserve his life and what remains of his health. In his home in Alexandria, Virginia, Bailes can have a low-stress, smoke-free environment that is genuinely therapeutic." The motion recounted a horrifying (and yet somehow inescapably comical) medical story about a *third* automobile accident, in July 1985, in which "Bailes's head was struck with such force that part of a dental plate was broken and swallowed. The sharp piece of metal lodged in his intestines, tearing them and ultimately causing peritonitis"—which, in turn, led to the onset of staphylococcus pneumonia. We would seem to be back in the world of the Hall of Fame and the barrel of nails that fell off the truck—were it not for the sheaf of hospital charts, physicians' reports, bills for drugs and surgical procedures, and insurance forms that Sheila appended to the motion as exhibits to confirm the story in all its preposterous and horrendous detail.

But one day, while perusing one of these exhibits—the attending physician's report on an insurance form—my attention was caught by an irregularity in one of the words the physician, Frank R. Crantz, M.D., of Fairview Hospital in Fairfax, Virginia, had used several times in his typewritten answers to the printed form's questions. The word was "swallowed" ("Patient swallowed a bridge . . . "), and I saw that in every case it had originally been typed "swollowed" and then corrected with a small pen stroke that transformed the "o"s into "a"s. I suddenly knew, as well as I knew anything, that Bailes had written the report. I recognized his manual typewriter and his writing style, as one recognizes a face. "Patient swallowed a bridge (from the mouth with one tooth on it, and a wire on it)," the con artist wrote, and went on, "which took 65 days to pass out of system, and as a direct result of the bridge being taken in intestine, he developed peritonitis, then in weakened condition developed staph pneumonia." I could almost feel Bailes's presence in the room with me and see the mischievous, perhaps even admiring, smile on his face as he acknowledged his authorship and my cleverness. I sent Dr. Crantz the form and asked him if he had written it. He called back to say that although he had no recollection of the case after so many years, he did know that no typewriter he had ever had in his office could have produced the typing on the form. "I'm an old English major, and this is not the way I write," he added. But, unexpectedly, he said that the signature looked like his own. It was not unheard-of at his hospital, he explained, for a patient to fill out the physician's part of an insurance form and then give it to the physician for his signature; no doubt, this is what happened here. So, once again, things grow misty and ambiguous and inconclusive, as all things with Bailes do.

For Sheila, however, it was clear as day that Bailes was one of life's unfortunates, a man with an unfair share of afflictions, for whom allowances must be made and to whom she must continue to minister, at whatever personal cost, if she was to continue to think of herself as a good person. As I read her motion—in which pity alternated with outrage—I was interested to note the appearance of Dr. C. Robert Meloni, a specialist in endocrinology and diabetes, whose diagnosis of hypercalcemia was to figure so prominently in Bailes's insanity defense at the Charlotte trial (as well as in the hearing before Judge Turk). Here Sheila merely mentioned the "cognitive dysfunction" that hypercalcemia caused, and moved on. She had enough on her plate with the three automobile accidents. (In a footnote, she cited an incredible fourth accident, a two-car collision near Abingdon in March 1986, in which Bailes suffered further head injuries, which "undoubtedly contributed to his inability to communicate his medical history to counsel." When I asked Sheila if she didn't think it astounding that Bailes had been in four—possibly even five, as yet another document suggested—car wrecks in two years, the question did not seem to have meaning for her.) The motion went on to protest the high calcium content of the water Bailes was obliged to drink in the Allenwood prison (not good for someone with too much calcium in his blood) and the prison's disregard for the dietary requirements of his diabetes. "At Allenwood, or at any other Bureau of Prisons facility, he is not free to go to the kitchen for a snack at any hour."

The authority figures before whom Bailes appeared all assumed that his physical symptoms were as fake as his insurance charters: the one followed from the other. Sheila, with comparable illogic, assumed that since Bailes's illnesses were genuine, so were his business dealings. It seems to have occurred to neither side that he could be at once a con man and a sick man. The old idea of illness as punishment for wrongdoing remains lodged in the collective unconscious but is selective in its exemplars: hypercalcemia as punishment for giving a false Social Security number to a bank somehow doesn't deliver the mythic punch that AIDS as punishment for buggery does. Debra Stuart's comment that Bailes's "physical difficulties are self-imposed" expresses the general consensus. It was simply assumed that when Bailes cried wolf, no beast was at his throat, and that Sheila's struggles with it were but another pantomime in his traveling snake-oil show.

After lunch, we stopped at Sheila's house to pick up some documents for me to take to New York. The parents were away. Their health was in a moment of precarious stability. Irene had had a cancerous growth removed from her face a few weeks earlier; Tom had had more heart trouble; but they were holding their own. Sheila's work as an office temporary gave her the freedom to drive her parents to and from Johns Hopkins Hospital in Baltimore for their appointments with their "top" doctors. Her professional ruin allowed her to play the role of the unmarried daughter who lives at home and cares for her aged parents—a role she adopted with complete naturalness and uncomplaining ardor.

Shortly before it was time for Sheila to drive me back to the station (I had long ago stopped protesting that I could call a taxi), the parents returned, and a consultation between mother and daughter was held in the front hall about providing me with something to carry my stack of documents in. Several candidates were considered, and finally a certain red canvas tote bag was chosen; Sheila went upstairs to fetch it. The incident struck me at the time, and has stayed in my mind, as the hallmark of a rare kind of domestic intimacy. Each woman knew exactly which tote bag was meant and where it was kept, and whether its condition was such that it could be loaned to a stranger without disgrace. When I mailed it back a day later, I felt sure it would be carefully returned to its place in an upstairs closet. I myself had never been upstairs. On my first visit, after Sheila's tour of the downstairs rooms, I had asked if I could see her room, and she had said, "Oh, no, it's too messy." Most of us would have said the same. We live under the delusion that we keep our congenital disorderliness hidden from the world. A moment's reflection (or the reading of a few pages of a novel) will tell us that we are constantly showing each other our messy inner rooms. Sheila had shown me hers without reserve; by now I knew it the way a mother knows the daughter's room that she passes every day, often with a sigh.

On the drive to the station, Sheila spoke of "a couple of character flaws that I have had all my life and still have, and that were probably brought into higher relief when I practiced law."

"What are these flaws?" I asked.

"I've always been quick to take offense and quick to give offense. I'm abrasive. And if you haven't seen too much of that side of me, it's because I see you as somebody who is helping me and is willing to listen to me. So, obviously, I try not to irritate you."

Sheila had never before referred to our relationship so directly. I hastened to push my way through the door that had opened slightly. "I feel bad about my impatience," I said. "The way I interrupt and argue with you."

"Oh, no, you've been extraordinarily patient—"

I cut in, "All those times when I've said, 'Now, Sheila, *come on.*'"

"Oh, no, that's just being a facilitator."

I kept it up. "I have felt like a bully."

"Oh, no, on the contrary." But then it was over. Sheila hustled me out the door and closed it firmly. "When I worked at Carnegie, I was all business," she said, back on the solid ground of the unilateral. "From the time I was twenty-seven, I had the responsibility of negotiating contracts for the institution, and I got rid of some of the people who had provided services for us. 'I'll put this out for bids,' I said. I was cold. I was pretty cold in business. And I was abrasive in my law practice, though I think it only fair to say—because I don't want to give you a picture that's inaccurate—that I didn't just come in and say, 'Okay, my client didn't do it. There is no evidence for it. You have to dismiss this charge.' Of course I tried to be pleasant, I tried to make my case personally to the state prosecutor. I tried to persuade him. Sometimes I was able to get good deals for my clients because I played the violin. It wasn't that I was always abrasive."

What Sheila had condescended to do for her indigent clients, she would not stoop to do for herself. She would not play the violin to get a good deal for herself from a journalist. She would try not to irritate me, but that's as far as she would go. Over the months of writing this book, my admiration and affection for her have grown. She has settled into my imagination as an exquisite heroine. The wrongness of her conviction and imprisonment is as distinct in my mind as the Elite font of Bailes's manual typewriter. And the heedless selflessness that propelled her downfall has thrown into relief the radicalism of her vision of defense law as a calling for the incorrigibly loyal. When I think of Sheila, I am awed by her disdain for the disguises for self-interest that the world offers us so it can get its business done. But when I speak with her on the telephone, my old irritation and impatience abruptly return. The conversations pain me, and I call as infrequently as possible. There is not much left for me to ask. I have mastered the incoherent and senseless story of her ruin. I know it in all its chaotic detail. I probably understand it about as well as anyone on earth does. But like Sheila's defeated defenders in law, I know I haven't saved her with my journalist's brief. I know that she still lies drowning in dark, weedy water—and that I must come up for air.

# CODA

THE SEPTEMBER day on which I visited William Sheffield in Abingdon was an outstandingly beautiful one, and, on an impulse, after parting from him I drove out of town to try to retrace the trip around the countryside I had made in the rain with Strother Smith the previous April. The landscape had radically changed. There was now a lush greenness everywhere; only the slant of the sun and an occasional, almost subliminal, yellowing in the hedgerows spoke of the end of summer. I was completely unsuccessful in my quest for another glimpse of the mirage of Winterham, nor could I find my way to the house in Glade Spring where Bailes lived with his first wife and their daughter. But some intuition led me back to Treasure Mountain. At first I wasn't sure—I rather doubted—that I had stumbled upon the right place. In the September greenness, the hillside was no longer bleak and unkempt. The little houses built by the bank no longer seemed contemptible; now trees and shrubs in full leaf blunted the architectural crassness so cruelly revealed in April's austerity. The houses looked agreeable and cared for, and the hillside had become an attractive stretch of wooded country.

As I ascended the hill along a road with pines, I recalled Strother Smith's saying that the trees were one of the few traces of Bailes still left on the property: Bailes had planted them in one of his spurts of enterprise, before the inevitable collapse.

The pines would be twenty-five years old now; they were handsome and soon would need thinning to remain so. Back in April, they had not seemed handsome; they had only brought the bleakness of the bare-boughed hillside into relief, as evergreens perversely do in early spring. Now, as part of the great general greening, they had come into their own.

I passed the place where Strother Smith had turned back and continued my ascent. Just below the top, I was rewarded by the sight of an ancient farm that had somehow survived Bailes, the bank, and who knows what other threats. There was a collection of weathered farm buildings, a field in which three horses grazed, gnarled apple trees, and, set back from the road, a small house with a porch and hanging ferns. A grape arbor abutted a garden (now dominated by nodding sunflowers), and miscellaneous items lay strewn about on the lawn (a canoe, some bicycles, a croquet set). I stopped the car to look at the house, and two dogs trotted over to bark in a routine and not unamiable manner. There was no one else on the place. I turned around and started back down the hill but stopped again, attracted by a pretty dappled glade where purple asters and goldenrod grew amidst spent jewelweed and joe-pye weed. I sat on the grass and wrote in my notebook about the sights I had just seen. The sound of crows broke, and then accentuated, the uncanny stillness one finds on mountains—even on those as small as Treasure Mountain.

A  NOTE  ON  THE  TYPE

THIS BOOK was set in Janson, a typeface long thought to have
been made by the Dutchman Anton Janson, who was a practicing typefounder in Leipzig during the years 1668 to 1687.
However, it has been conclusively demonstrated that these
types are actually the work of Nicholas Kis (1650–1702), a Hun-
garian, who most probably learned his trade from the master
Dutch typefounder Dirk Voskens. The type is an excellent
example of the influential and sturdy Dutch types that prevailed
in England up to the time William Caslon (1692–1766) developed his own incomparable designs from them.

Composed by Stratford Publishing Services,
Brattleboro, Vermont
Printed and bound by R. R. Donnelley & Sons,
Harrisonburg, Virginia
Designed by Virginia Tan